WINNING SHOPPING CENTER DESIGNS

No. 2

WINNING SHOPPING CENTER DESIGNS
No. 2

RETAIL REPORTING CORP., NEW YORK

Retail Reporting Corporation
302 Fifth Avenue
New York, NY 10001

Distributors to the trade in the United States and Canada
McGraw-Hill, Inc
1221 Avenue of the Americas
New York, NY 10020

Distributors outside the United States and Canada
Hearst Books International
1350 Avenue of the Americas
New York, NY 10019

Library of Congress Cataloging in Publication Data:
Winning Shopping Center Designs / 2

Printed in Hong Kong
ISBN 0-934590-75-3

Text Design: Harish Patal Design

Contents

Foreword

A total of 47 entries were submitted to the International Council of Shopping Centers 1995 International Design and Development Awards competition, including entries from Canada, Australia, Japan, Singapore and Indonesia. There were 32 entries in the category of "Renovation or Expansion of an Existing Project" and 15 entries in the category of "Innovative Design and Construction of a New Project."

The individual committee members came from a diversity of backgrounds encompassing retailing, architecture, development, consultancy and institutional asset management. Each of the entries was evaluated on the basis of five separate criteria: presentation of entry materials; combination of color, materials and lighting; design — interior and exterior; overall development goal; and degree of difficulty and innovation. The committee worked with intensity to analyze and evaluate the submissions, and the results satisfied all of the constituencies.

You might be interested to know that "innovational" is defined under Scottish law as "the renewal of an obligation to pay." These innovative designs truly reflect a sense of obligation to customers and retailers to develop a product that is both pleasing and exciting. As you review this book, I think you will share our enthusiasm for the remarkable creativity and exceptional expertise demonstrated in these projects.

Milton Cooper
Kimco Realty Corporation

Chairman
ICSC 1995 International Design and Development Awards

About the ICSC International Design and Development Awards

The ICSC International Design and Development Awards Program was established to recognize outstanding shopping center projects and to provide information on them to the entire industry so that others may benefit from the experiences of their colleagues.

The 1995 International Design and Development Awards Program was worldwide in scope. Participation in other ICSC Design Awards Programs, such as the Canadian or European Awards, did not preclude eligible projects from being considered for an International Design and Development Award.

This was the 19th year of the program. Projects opened within the 18th-month period, January 1, 1993 to June 30, 1994, were eligible for entry into this year's Awards Program.

Awards Categories

Categories for entries were:

Category A—Renovation or Expansion of an Existing Project
Entries had to relate to a project involving an entire shopping center, such as an enclosure, or a single facet of a center, as in an addition. The renovation or expansion must have been completed and the center fully opened for business within the 18-month period, January 1, 1993 to June 30, 1994. Eligible subject matter included, but was not limited to, improving the use of existing space, methods of keeping a center open during construction, new marketing and re-leasing approaches, refinancing techniques, innovative design and construction approaches, and adaptive reuse of the structure.

Category B—Innovative Design and Construction of a New Project
Entries had to relate to a specific new shopping center, completed and opened within the 18-month period, January 1, 1993 to June 30, 1994, and must have demonstrated how a specific design or construction problem was solved or how new standards in design or construction were established. New methods of environmental enhancement, space utilization design themes, energy conservation, and innovative construction techniques were among the subjects that were considered for this category. Entries included detailed information about the design and construction of the center, such as explanations of the reasons for, and the realized accomplishments of, the particular approach.

Awards Classifications

Entries submitted for either **category** were judged according to the following center **classification** system:

1. Projects under 150,000 square feet of total retail space*
2. Projects of 150,001 to 500,000 square feet of total retail space*
3. Projects over 500,001 square feet of total retail space.*

*Total retail space includes all square footage included in gross leasable areas (GLA), all department store or other anchor square footage, movie theaters, ice skating rinks, entertainment centers, and all peripheral (out-lot) space engaged in retail enterprise. It does not include office or hotel square footage.

Eligibility

1. The ICSC International Design and Development Awards Program was open only to ICSC member companies. Any ICSC member company could enter as many projects as desired in either of the two categories.
2. Entries must have had the authorization and signature of the owner or management company of the property.
3. Projects opened within the 18-month period, January 1, 1993 to June 30, 1994, were eligible.
4. Projects must have been completed and opened for business by June 30, 1994.
5. Separate phases of a project could be submitted individually, provided they were completed and opened for business by June 30, 1994.
6. Projects could only be submitted once. Projects that were entered in the past could not be resubmitted unless substantial changes were made since the last submission.
7. Members entering the ICSC Canadian or ICSC European Awards Programs had to submit separately to the International Design and Development Awards Program and entries had to adhere to its entry guidelines and requirements. Entries accepted to other ICSC awards programs did not automatically qualify for this program, nor was any entry excluded simply because it was an award winner in another program.

If you have any questions about the International Council of Shopping Centers International Design and Development Awards or would like to receive an application for the upcoming awards program, please write or call:

International Council of
Shopping Centers
International Design and
Development Awards
665 Fifth Avenue
New York, NY 10022-5370
Telephone: (212) 421-8181, ext. 320
FAX: (212) 486-0849

Acknowledgments

The International Council of Shopping Centers 1995 Design and Development Awards were selected by a committee of diverse shopping center professionals representing retailers, developers, and architects. The International Council of Shopping Centers is grateful to these judges for the time, effort, and expertise they contributed to the awards program.

Milton Cooper, *Chairman*
Kimco Realty Corporation
New Hyde Park, New York

Ronald A. Altoon, FAIA
Altoon + Porter Architects
Los Angeles, California

Stanley C. Burgess
The Rouse Company
Columbia, Maryland

Gordon T. Greeby
The Greeby Companies, Inc.
Vernon Hills, Illinois

Michael Lowenkron
JC Penney Co., Inc.
Dallas, Texas

Daryl K. Mangan
Equitable R. E. Investment Management, Inc.
Atlanta, Georgia

Richard E. Montag
The Richard E. Jacobs Group
New York, New York

Ian F. Thomas
Thomas Consultants, Inc.
Vancouver, British Columbia

Gerald M. White
Copaken, White & Blitt
Leawood, Kansas

Innovative Design and Construction of a New Project

Innovative Design and Construction Of a New Project

Owner:
Keenan/Bariteau Partners, L.P.
Palo Alto, California

Architect:
Kenneth Rodrigues Associates
San Jose, California

Designers:
Kenneth Rodrigues, Architect, and
Sussman/Prejza & Co., Inc.
San Jose, California

Design Award

Main Street at Santa Teresa

San Jose, California United States

Gross size of center:
138,494 sq. ft.

Gross leasable area excluding anchors:
88,309 sq. ft.

Total acreage of site:
11.12 acres

Type of center:
Neighborhood center

Physical description:
One-level strip center

Location of trading area:
Suburban

Population:
- Primary trading area
  174,000
- Secondary trading area
  354,000

Development schedule:
- Present center

  Date opened
  June 1994

Parking spaces:
- Present number
  620

A villagelike appearance permeates Main Street at Santa Teresa.

Tony & Alba's
PIZZA PASTA
SCORE
NOW OPEN

Location and a neighborhood-sensitive lobbying campaign on the part of the shopping center developer were the key components of success for Main Street at Santa Teresa, a neighborhood shopping center in San Jose.

The vacant property, originally zoned for high-density residential development, was owned by an insurance company that had been unsuccessful for 25 years in persuading the City Council to rezone the site for retail use. It was also located diagonally across from a regional mall. The city planner firmly believed that the property must be reserved for residential use.

Entry pylons designed in a variety of styles communicate the individual identities of the major stores.

Eye-catching signage calls attention to Main Street's retailers.

The Main Street developer, however, learned that the community wanted a high-quality community shopping center on at least a portion of the property, and the prospects boded well. Apart from the presence of the mall, the site was the last remaining large parcel in the area suitable for commercial use. Traffic counts at the intersection of Blossom Hill Road and Santa Teresa Boulevard exceeded 90,000 cars per day.

Gathering the community's support became the first priority in development. The overall design of the center, the developer reports, was strongly influenced by community opinion.

Approximately half of the total 23-acre site was reserved for what has become a 320-unit apartment complex.

The one-level strip center did not sacrifice architectural detail.

MAJOR TENANTS

NAME	TYPE	GLA (SQ. FT.)
Lucky Stores	Supermarket	50,185
Super Crown Books	Bookstore	15,347
Blockbuster Music	Music store	14,082
Kinko's Copies	Printing/copying	6,377

A New Street for Retail

The principal design problem for the project was siting the major anchor, a Lucky Stores supermarket, and orienting the center to two major street frontages, Blossom Hill Road and Santa Teresa Boulevard. Historically, Blossom Hill Road had been the desired retail address in the area. Two new freeways were under construction while the center was in the approval process, however. The intersection of these freeways was only a quarter-mile north of the center site, and Santa Teresa Boulevard would be the city street extension of one of them. The developers believed that the new freeway link would give Santa Teresa Boulevard equal stature to Blossom Hill Road as a retail location, and indeed, the stores facing Santa Teresa Boulevard were the first leased at Main Street.

The overall layout of Main Street at Santa Teresa is an unusual "reverse U." The Lucky Stores supermarket faces the corner of Blossom Hill Road and Santa Teresa Boulevard. Small tenants face one street or the other.

Signage and awnings are individually designed at many of Main Street's stores.

The center's plan shows how the "reverse U" faces two major arteries.

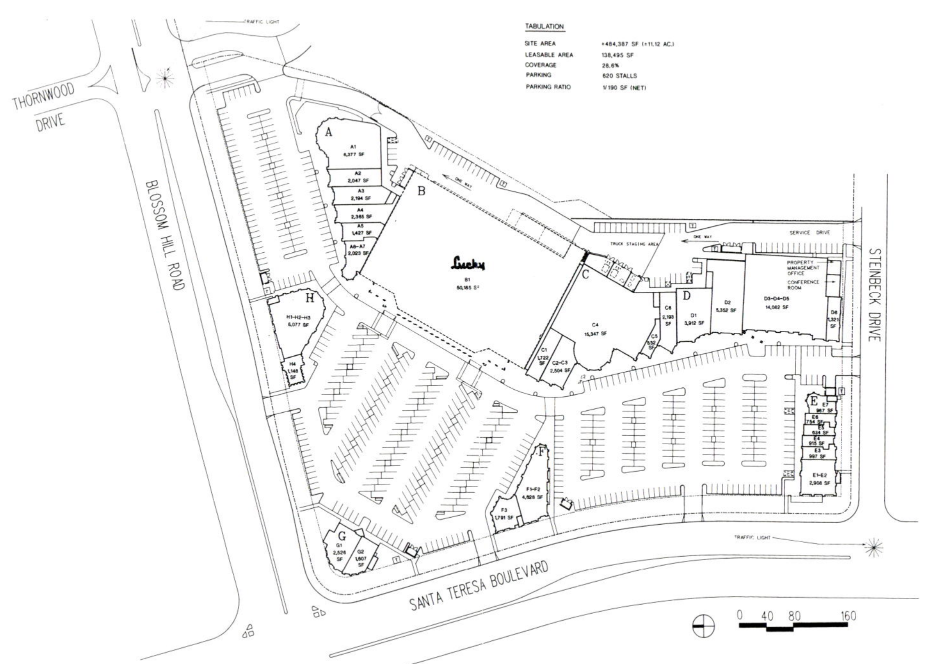

Store facades are varied, emphasizing retailers' individualities.

Design Elements

Signage plays a key role in the retailers' success. Individually crafted signs were created for virtually all tenants and are emphasized by a variety of exterior colors and awning treatments.

Where possible, the developer permitted modifications to the original design elevations during the construction process, allowing a tenant to present its image in a more striking manner. The varied store facades are also emphasized by enlarged common-area sidewalks, reminding shoppers of the "Main Street" theme. Generous outside seating areas were created to take advantage of the mild climate.

Looking back, the developer only regrets underestimating retailers' demand for the site and believes that the remaining 12 acres (now containing the apartment complex) could have attracted national retailers that have not yet been able to locate in the San Jose area. Still, developer and retailers alike report that the time spent marshaling community support for the center and Main Street at Santa Teresa's design execution have paid off handsomely in rental rates, occupancy levels and sales figures.

Circular buildings create a unique look for a strip center.

Colorful landscaping is the crowning design touch for Main Street at Santa Teresa.

Innovative Design and Construction Of a New Project

Owner:
Homart
Chicago, Illinois

Architect/Designer:
ELS/Elbasani & Logan Architects
Berkeley, California

Design Award

North Point Mall

Alpharetta, Georgia United States

Gross size of center:
1,115,102 sq. ft.

Gross leasable area excluding anchors:
397,000 sq. ft.

Total acreage of site:
103 acres

Type of center:
Superregional mall

Physical description:
Enclosed two-level mall

Location of trading area:
Suburban

Population:
- Primary trading area 312,000

Development schedule:
- Present center

  Date opened
  October 20, 1993
- Future expansion:

  Anticipated date
  Spring 1996 (Dillard's)

Parking spaces:
- Present number 6,591
- Number to be added 530

Elevators in North Point Mall have counterweight sculptures that rise and fall in counterpoint to the movement of the elevator cage.

North Point Mall faced a dual challenge as design work began. The mall lay 40 feet lower than Georgia Highway 400, its major vehicular feed, and city government had mandated a tree protection zone 120 feet deep. It was essential to create an architectural image for North Point Mall that could be seen from the highway.

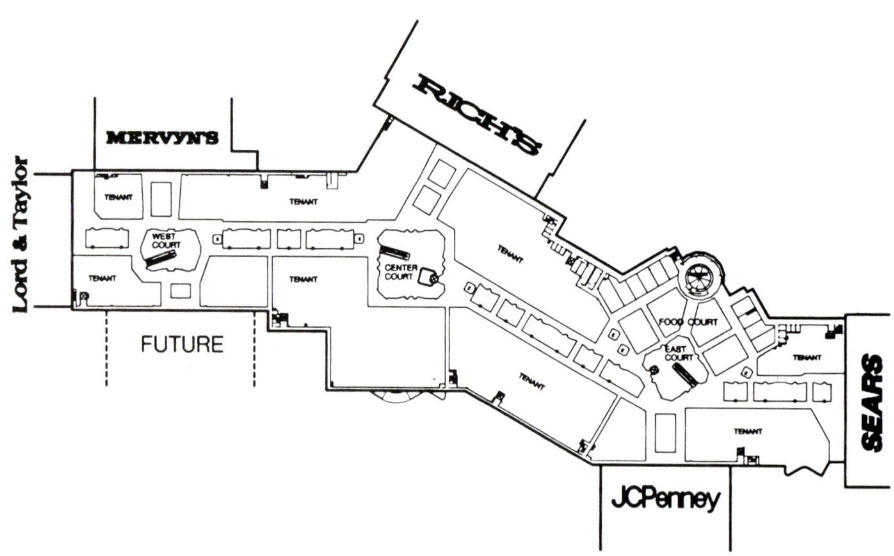

North Point Mall's new layout places each anchor off a court and leaves a pad for a fifth major tenant.

Masts reaching through the skylit roof to a height of 85 feet are a principal design statement.

Exterior Design

Nineteen 85-foot-high masts linked by cables supporting a skylit vaulted roof punctuated by three pyramidal cupolas made North Point Mall into a striking skyline from Georgia Highway 400. Nighttime lighting transforms the entire length of the building into a sequence of shimmering beacons. The lightweight supporting cables provide both structural and design support by helping to pull the roof toward the masts, thus creating an asymmetrical ceiling configuration over interior walkways.The 85-foot-high masts pierce the continuous northern skylight and end at the mall's lower level.

Interior Elements

Inside, elegant architectural detailing permeates railings, floor patterns and the lacy filigree of metalwork on street lamps. The elevators add a dimension of surprise through counterweight sculptures that rise and fall in counterpoint to the movement of the elevator cage.

North Point's pyramidal cupolas and steel masts create a new nighttime skyline in the Atlanta suburbs.

MAJOR TENANTS

NAME	TYPE	GLA (SQ. FT.)
Rich's	Department store	240,000
Mervyn's	Department store	83,560
Sears	Department store	154,886
JC Penney	Department store	124,656
Lord & Taylor	Department store	115,000
Dillard's (1996)	Department store	249,000

The visual impact of the masts is integrated at entry markers and elsewhere throughout the mall.

Metalwork filigree gives an air of elegance to North Point Mall.

The counterweight sculpture rises and falls as the elevator brings shoppers to other levels.

The "Greening" of North Point

As extraordinary as it may be, North Point's design is just one of the mall's benefits to its community, which has an average household income of $72,000 and a median age of 34. Nine acres of wetland adjacent to the mall have been preserved. Over 1,400 pine trees were planted along Georgia Highway 400. Within the ring road, 43,000 shrubs, ground cover plants and trees were planted to maintain the lush natural look of the surroundings.

Curvilinear flooring patterns are done on a grand scale.

Accent lighting defines the soaring masts each evening.

One of three pyramidal skylights at North Point Mall.

A terrace adjacent to the food court and in view of the carousel provides outdoor seating and a smoking area.

Success Indicators

The success of the center is evident in the fact that the name "North Point" is being incorporated into the names of businesses along the Georgia Highway 400 growth corridor. The mall has not only stimulated that growth but makes its own major contribution to it. North Point Mall opened with 88 percent small-tenant occupancy in October 1993 and commitments for an additional four percent — an opening-day leasing rate hard to match in recent years.

The mall's dramatic design attracted many of those tenants and brought in not only area shoppers but also patrons from distances farther away than marketing studies had anticipated.

Owner:
New River Associates
c/o Westcor Realty L.P.
Phoenix, Arizona

Architect:
Omniplan Architects
Dallas, Texas

Designer:
Mark Dilworth, AIA
Omniplan Architects
Dallas, Texas

Certificate of Merit

Arrowhead Towne Center

Glendale, Arizona United States

Gross size of center:
1,313,829 sq. ft.

Gross leasable area excluding anchors:
230,000 sq. ft.

Total acreage of site:
100 acres

Type of center:
Superregional center

Physical description:
Enclosed two-level mall

Population:
- Primary trading area
  230,000

Development schedule:
- Present center

  Date opened
  October 1993

Parking spaces:
- Present number
  5,805

Orange-capped towers greet shoppers at Arrowhead Towne Center.

Arrowhead Towne Center is the centerpiece of a planned 600-acre mixed-use development that will eventually be half retail and half a combination of office, industrial, residential and recreational uses.

As the first phase of the mixed-use project, Arrowhead Towne Center benefited from a close working relationship between the developer and officials of the City of Glendale.

The design reflects the mall's Southwest desert surroundings. Exteriors mix local colors with dark purples and oranges. Approaching shoppers are greeted by a cactus garden and a fountain.

A cactus garden greets shoppers at Arrowhead Towne Center.

Visitors to the grassy amphitheater may be reminded of Stonehenge as they gaze at a water feature.

A computerized water feature contrasts with the arid desert soil.

The main court combines strong floor patterns, airiness, natural light and eye-catching art (opposite).

MAJOR TENANTS		
NAME	TYPE	GLA (SQ. FT.)
Dillard's	Department store	204,000
Robinson's-May	Department store	190,500
JC Penney	Department store	140,000
Montgomery Ward	Department store	120,000
Mervyn's	Department store	82,000

Color and Light

Interiors are kept to off-white shades with bright visual splashes from large suspended sculptures. The exposed steel frame is painted in desert colors. Floor patterns are based on Indian rug designs. A great deal of natural light is used. A roof pyramid at center court brings to mind the green peaks of nearby mountains.

Objectives of Layout

Mall layout sought to achieve two key goals. First, the developer aimed to create the strongest possible flow of shoppers throughout the maximum length of the mall. This goal was achieved by placing the five anchor stores at the far ends of the mall, thus eliminating weak traffic areas. A second goal, to make the food court an integral part of the mall, was accomplished by placing it at center court and adjacent to the cinema and outdoor amphitheater.

ROBINSON'S-MAY
FUTURE DEPARTMENT STORE
MERVYN'S
Cinema Under Construction
MONTGOMERY WARD
JC PENNEY
DILLARDS

LOWER LEVEL PLAN

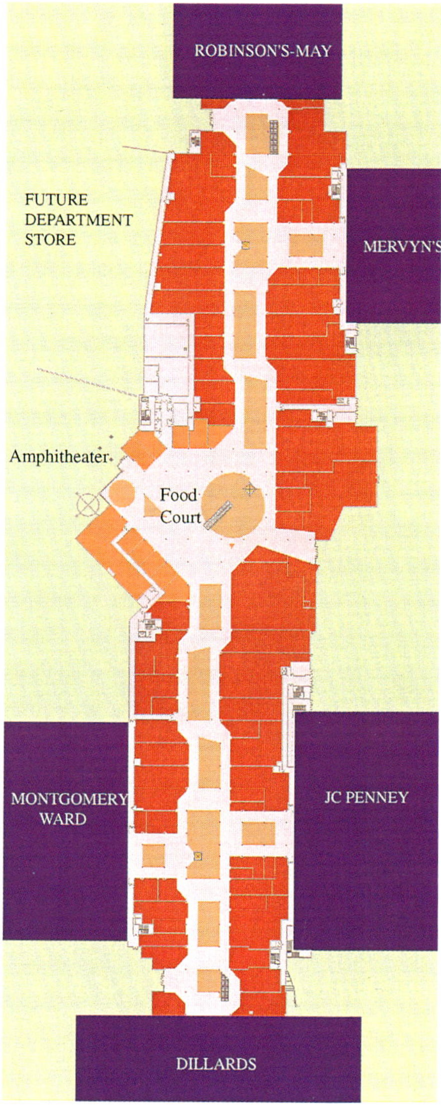

UPPER LEVEL PLAN

Anchors were placed at the far ends of the mall to maximize traffic flow throughout the length of the mall.

Natural light and stylish lamps brighten a shopping visit to Arrowhead Towne Center.

The mall layout features offsets to give the stores more "merchandising corners."

Attention to Retailers

Tenant needs were anticipated throughout the planning. Offsets in the layout of the mall walkway give stores more "merchandising corners." Mall store depths were kept to 80 feet or less. Anchors benefit from high visibility from all road systems. Space was left for the addition of a sixth anchor store.

Sculptures hang from the industrial-style roof, lending aesthetics to the technological look.

Innovative Design and Construction Of a New Project

Owner:
Thakral Holdings Limited
Sydney, New South Wales
Australia

Architect:
Buchan Laird & Bawden
Melbourne, Victoria
Australia

Designer:
Buchan Laird & Bawden
Melbourne, Victoria
Australia

Australia on Collins

Melbourne, Victoria Australia

Gross size of center:
87,393 sq. ft.

Gross leasable area excluding anchors:
83,309 sq. ft.

Total acreage of site:
1.02 acres

Type of center:
Multi-use/Fashion center

Physical description:
Enclosed fourteen-level atrium (five mall levels plus nine hotel levels)

Location of trading area:
Urban central business district

Population:
- Primary trading area 100,000+
- Secondary trading area 3,400,000

Development schedule:
- Present center

  Date opened
  February 1993

Parking spaces:
- Present number
  No on-site parking

The center's five-level atrium expands to fourteen levels when the attached Novotel Hotel, with an entry on the center's uppermost retail level, is included.

In Melbourne's central city retail district, Australia on Collins transformed a 50-year-old retail arcade with hotel and restaurant into a high-quality mixed-use development containing 53 specialty stores, 4 restaurants and a 17-unit food court around a 14-level atrium.

The site extends through one city block (about 110 yards) and forms part of a pedestrian arcade spine connecting a main mass transit rail station with high-quality retail stores, specialty stores and department stores. The Australia on Collins site had once been a successful center but had been allowed to run down to little more than a pedestrian racetrack for 26,000 daily commuters.

The design challenge for the Australia on Collins development team was to take advantage of this large traffic flow and encourage people to circulate through the new center's various levels.

A facade of shimmering glass is the first attraction to Australia on Collins.

Escalators move shoppers to upper retail levels.

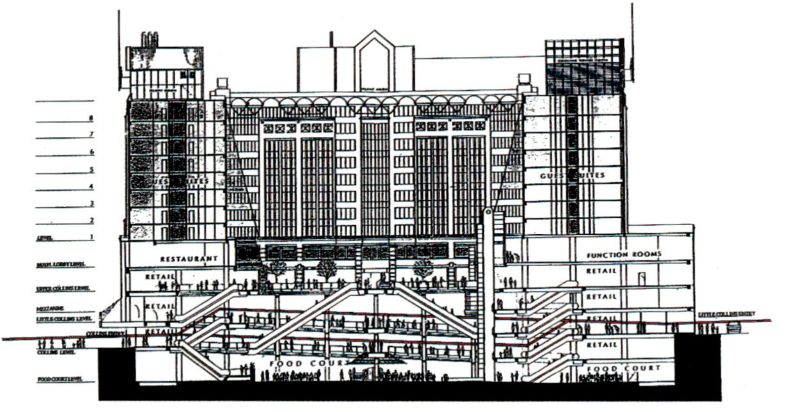

The scale of the 14-level atrium is evident at this elevator tower.

Stores are clearly visible from the street, inviting pedestrians to become shoppers.

A "Manhattan" theme complements one area of the food court.

Working With the Authorities

Considerable obstacles faced the developers. The National Trust Preservation Society would need to reverse its continuing objection to redevelopment. Government would not allow on-site parking and required the project to be compatible in form, scale and character with nearby historic buildings.

Center Levels

Circulation through the center posed special challenges that ultimately presented unique opportunities. The old center had a 3-foot 6-inch fall as one passed from north to south through the building. The Collins Street and Little Collins Street entrance levels were gently ramped contrary to the fall, thus creating two principal ground floor retail levels. Five street entrances were exactly aligned with entrances to adjacent arcades, creating a traffic flow from block to block.

The lowest level includes a themed food court, restaurant and bar, with seating for 900 people. This level opens each morning two hours before the retail stores, with the bar and some eateries open in the evenings as well.

The food court is visible from many retail levels and from escalators.

The uppermost retail level became "Collins Street in the Sky," recreating the ambience of old Collins Street with strong retail stores, a sidewalk café and exhibition space. This level has an entrance to the nine-level Novotel Hotel, whose most favored guest rooms overlook the atrium.

Introducing Foreign Retailers

Tenant mix was developed carefully and creatively to bring to Australia on Collins retailers from other parts of Australia and other countries, thus distinguishing its tenant mix from that of suburban regional malls.

Construction Demands

Conventional structural and construction techniques were generally used throughout the project, but basement construction was complicated by varying difficult conditions in adjacent buildings.

The strong design statement of the mall also informs the hotel entrance.

Imaginative and elegant storefronts introduce retail into a commuter's trip (below and opposite).

MAJOR TENANTS		
NAME	**TYPE**	**GLA (SQ. FT.)**
Lincraft	Fashion and furnishing fabrics	17,673
Country Road	Fashion, gifts, homeware	7,842
Food court	17 units	N/A

An Active Public Place

Australia on Collins has achieved its goal of becoming an active public place, partly due to the strong retail presence and food court, but also to the attractiveness of the interior design. Public area materials, finishes, detailing, colors and lighting are of high quality. Special lighting was installed to create an "after-dark" ambience as well.

Melbourne had become a scene of 80 empty street-level retail stores in the downtown core area. Yet despite the economic downturn, Australia on Collins opened on time, on budget, fully leased, with the hotel operating, to high acclaim from the public and the Australian property industry.

Owner:
Intershop Real Estate Services, Inc.
Dallas, Texas

Architect:
Davis Fredrikson Davis
Phoenix, Arizona

Designer:
Michael R. Davis, AIA
Phoenix, Arizona

Certificate of Merit

Mesa Fiesta Power Center

Mesa, Arizona United States

Gross size of center:
205,500 sq. ft.

Gross leasable area excluding anchors:
193,000 sq. ft.

Total acreage of site:
18 acres

Type of center:
Power center

Physical description:
One-level center

Location of trading area:
Suburban

Population:
- Primary trading area
  335,000
- Secondary trading area
  703,000

Development schedule:
- Present center

  Date opened
  March 1, 1994

Parking spaces:
- Present number
  998

The colors of the desert are incorporated into the signage at Mesa Fiesta Power Center.

MESA
FIESTA

The developer of Mesa Fiesta Power Center sought to create a retail center that was sensitive to the needs of its neighborhood and would serve not only as a shopping destination but also as a community gathering place for such functions as concerts and art exhibits.

The major retailers are visible to anyone parking in the Mesa Fiesta Power Center lot.

Zoned for high-rise office use, the 18-acre site had been described as the "jewel" piece of unoccupied land in Mesa, and its disposition was a much-discussed issue, requiring four zoning hearings for approval.

The land was very expensive, the developer said, and the project was financially viable only because the seven medium-sized "anchors" pay a higher rental rate than would a single larger tenant.

Desert tones provide a backdrop to stores' logos.

Four-Sided Exposure

Plans called for a single-story 205,000 sq. ft. center with seven major retailers, one "mini-major" (a discount shoe store) and two restaurant pads. The site has four-sided street exposure, making traditional loading dock areas inappropriate. Instead, architectural detail enhances all four sides. Even roof treatments were designed to be appealing sights for people in adjacent mid-rise offices and hotels.

Colored paving materials and columnar landscape elements serve as visual icons and screening devices. Loading dock areas are particularly well screened and landscaped.

Roof treatments (left) are designed to please viewers from neighboring offices and hotels.

Designers used shading structures to meet shoppers' need for relief from the Arizona sun (below).

Amphitheater and Store Structure

Mesa Fiesta has achieved its goal of becoming a community gathering place thanks to its 1.5-acre grass amphitheater with suspended shading structures built in between the two wings of the L-shaped center. The amphitheater also serves as a visual buffer between Mesa Fiesta and an adjacent hotel.

Each store is given an individual identity through varying parapet heights and pyramidal mechanical screens. Overall, the natural desert colors, low-profile buildings and simple geometric forms make Mesa Fiesta both distinctive and harmonious with its environment.

MAJOR TENANTS

NAME	TYPE	GLA (SQ. FT.)
Best Buy	Video/computer/appliance	40,000
Marshalls	Discount clothing	31,000
Borders Books	Bookstore	25,000
CompUSA	Computer	25,000
Linens Plus	Linens/kitchenware	25,000
Staples	Office supplies	20,000
Cost Plus	Imported goods/foods	20,000

Exterior sculpture and shade screens at the amphitheater make architectural statements (above and left).

Owner:
Cousins/New Market Development Company
Atlanta, Georgia

Architect/Designer:
Ogram Architects
Atlanta, Georgia

Certificate of Merit

Perimeter Expo

Atlanta, Georgia United States

Gross size of center:
170,755 sq. ft.

Gross leasable area excluding anchors:
15,929 sq. ft.

Total acreage of site:
10.42 acres

Type of center:
Power center

Physical description:
Two-level center

Location of trading area:
Suburban

Population:
- Primary trading area
  64,000
- Secondary trading area
  170,000

Development schedule:
- Present center

  Date opened
  October 30, 1993

Parking spaces:
- Present number
  1,325

Perimeter Expo's image is striking at twilight.

Marshalls
BEST BUY

Escalators are plainly visible from the parking lots.

MAJOR TENANTS		
NAME	**TYPE**	**GLA (SQ. FT.)**
Marshalls	Off-price	36,598
Best Buy	Off-price	36,090
Linens 'n Things	Off-price	30,351
Office Max	Off-price	23,500
The Sport Shoe	Off-price	14,348
Everything Organized	Off-price	13,939

A site plan and an aerial view show how Home Depot's building works with Perimeter Expo to create a unified retail presence.

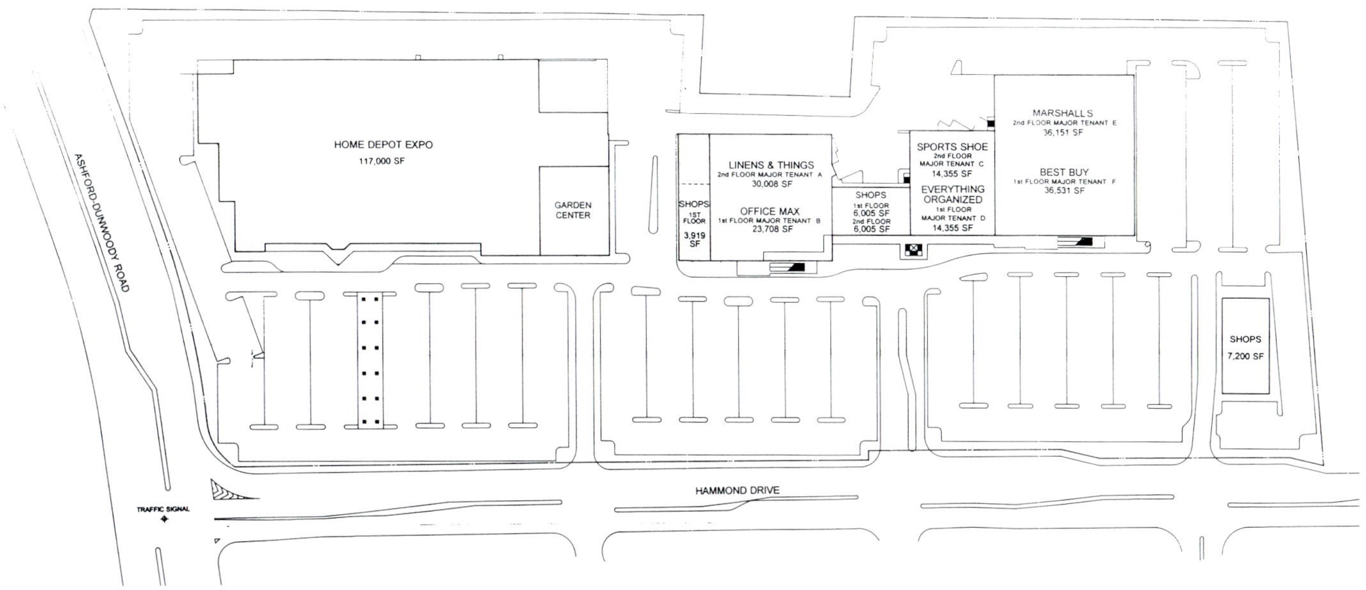

Dual challenges faced the developer of Perimeter Expo in an Atlanta suburb: meeting a five-month "fast track" construction schedule and making a two-story open-air center work for the retailers on the higher floor.

Perimeter Expo was sited next to the nation's second Home Depot Expo to create the area's first off-price shopping complex. Major tenant openings required completion nine months after the project's initiation, leaving only five months for base building and tenant construction. Concessions, the developer reports, were made by everyone. Site work was also performed by the owners of the adjacent Home Depot, requiring efficient coordination during the compressed construction period.

Photo courtesy Peter Fownes, © 1994.

Design Elements

Architectural design plays a large role in the center's success story. Glass was used extensively to maximize visibility and draw attention. The exterior features enlarged storefronts, custom handrails and a wall system composed of glass and white tubes that shelter the escalators and create a visual link between the two floors. At night, up-lighting and accent lighting draw attention to the entries, which also contain the escalators. Elements of the architectural design convey the ease of vertical circulation — a critical component — from vantage points as far away as the exterior roadway.

Store signage boldly announces the presence of strong retail on the upper floor.

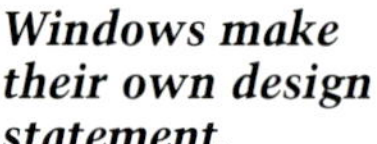

Windows make their own design statement.

Varying roof styles top anchor stores and escalator wells (above and below).

Anchor Architecture and Layout

The locations of major tenants are clearly communicated. Roof forms rise and fall to define their spaces. Different colors of brick differentiate major tenants from the shops. Synthetic limestone forms provide a heavy cornice over the major-tenant spaces. Finally, alternating domes and pyramids atop the majors, in concert with those over the adjacent escalator wells, create an eye-catching skyline.

The two-story layout required attracting major national tenants whose appeal would encourage the ride up the escalators. The developer found, however, that shoppers appreciated the compactness of the site: escalators "did" the walking or driving from store to store that usually accompanies shopping at large, spread-out power centers.

Openings

Construction was timed for the November/December holiday season. A June 2 construction start and on-site supervision by the developer led to Best Buy's opening on October 30, Marshalls' on November 19 and other openings at Thanksgiving and in early December.

The center was fully leased before opening and remains that way, with tenants performing well above projections, the developer reports. A mass transit station to be located nearby in 1996 promises a wider customer base as well.

Roofs provide protection from inclement weather.

Renovation or Expansion of an Existing Project

Renovation or Expansion of an Existing Project

Owner:
Clarke Quay Pte Ltd
Singapore

Local Architect:
RSP Architects Planners & Engineers
Singapore

Design Architect:
ELS/Elbasani & Logan Architects
Berkeley, California

Design Award

Clarke Quay

Singapore

Gross size of center:
226,876 sq. ft.

Amount of space added or renovated:
226,876 sq. ft.

Gross leasable area excluding anchors:
189,873 sq. ft.

Total acreage of site:
8.3 acres

Type of center:
Festival village

Physical description:
Shopping district

Location of trading area:
Urban central business district

Population:
- Primary trading area
  2,800,000
- Secondary trading area
  5,600,000

Development schedule:
Date opened
November 21, 1993

Parking spaces:
- Present number
  400

Clarke Quay shines at night.

Clarke Quay

Located in Singapore's central business district, along a tight bend in the Singapore River, the Clarke Quay district was in a state of severe deterioration in 1988. Numerous structures, abandoned for decades, were near collapse.

The government of Singapore had long sought to revitalize the district while maintaining the existing buildings' architectural design and the concepts of their original construction. Clarke Quay's redevelopers envisioned Singapore's first riverfront festival village, combining dining, shopping and entertainment uses. The resulting project contains 176 retail shops and over 20 restaurants and pubs, as well as an adventure ride celebrating Singapore's heritage and history through "100 Years on the Singapore River."

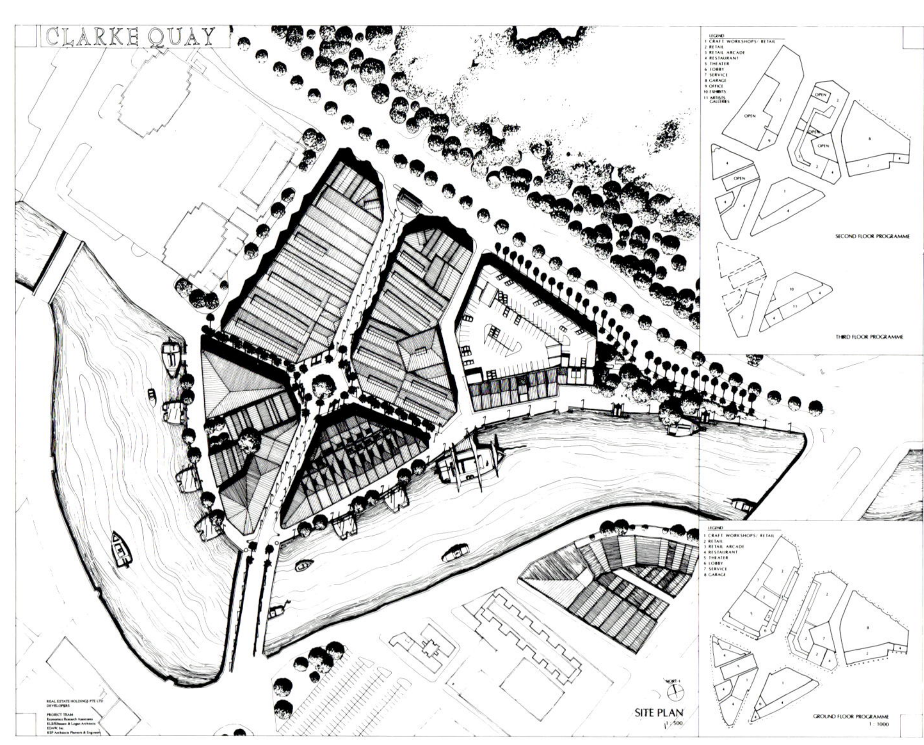

MAJOR TENANTS		
NAME	**TYPE**	**GLA (SQ. FT.)**
Clarke Quay Adventure	Adventure ride	28,976
Sogo	Department store	13,870
Wang Jiang Lou Yunnan Kitchen	Restaurant	11,098
B&N Fragrance	Fragrances and cosmetics	2,637
East India Company	Apparel	2,088

Clarke Quay sits beside a tight bend in the Singapore River.

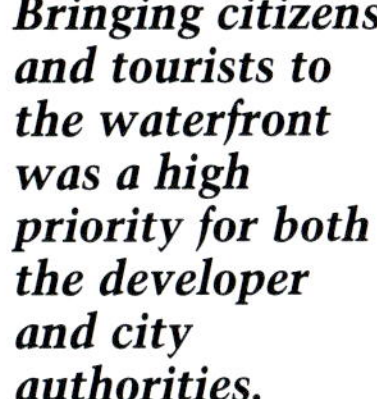

Bringing citizens and tourists to the waterfront was a high priority for both the developer and city authorities.

Government requirements for redevelopment were many. In addition to preserving the design and construction concepts of the original buildings, the Singapore Urban Redevelopment Authority (URA) mandated several new buildings on vacant lots within the district. The new and old buildings together were to form "an integrated shopping, entertainment, recreational and cultural development."

Traditional Materials Available

Historic facades were restored and interiors adapted. Traditional materials used in the original buildings, such as plaster, timber windows and shutters, and terra cotta tile roofing, are still in widespread use and are easily available. The use of contemporary materials was restrained to minimize the contrast between restored exteriors and new interiors.

Graphics and signage were inspired by traditional shophouse and warehouse sign types and styles. An extensive palette of muted, weathered colors was selected to avoid a bright "brand-new" look.

The Clarke Quay district was revitalized while maintaining the existing buildings' architectural design.

Upper levels of warehouses and shophouses, once used for offices and private family quarters, were modified to house specialty restaurants and clubs. New retail buildings and a parking structure were designed to complement rather than mimic their older neighbors in terms of proportion, scale and detailing.

The URA permitted some changes, however, including alterations in warehouses to create two levels of shopping and the adventure ride.

All parties sought to bring people to the riverfront, which was transformed into an active promenade. Large dining tongkang boats were moored at the river's edge. Many food vendors and restaurants opened in buildings along the quay. A 400-car parking garage was added behind existing shophouses.

The transformed riverfront is now a welcomed mooring place for boats.

Many food vendors opened in buildings in Clarke Quay.

Successful Adaptive Reuse

Successful strategies in the adaptive reuse of Clarke Quay included the closing of streets to traffic in order to create a pedestrian district and the use of a central mechanical plant to air condition the entire complex of buildings.

The project is continually being fine-tuned to strengthen the connections between inside and outside on the retail blocks (larger entries, greater tenant visibility, more signage). Government is now willing to allow these street-level changes. The redevelopers state that, in retrospect, they would have added more parking.

Clarke Quay stands in sharp contrast to recent developments elsewhere in Asia, where the old was razed and replaced by modern structures. It remains Singapore's largest single development and conservation project, and it spearheads a new commitment to the reuse of historic buildings. Clarke Quay has saved a piece of Singapore's priceless — and nearly lost — architectural and cultural heritage while bringing new economic and civic life to the once-abandoned riverfront district.

Closing of streets to traffic created a pedestrian district.

Renovation or Expansion of an Existing Project

Owner:
Green Hills Associates
Minneapolis, Minnesota

Architect:
Altoon + Porter Architects
Los Angeles, California

Design Award

The Mall at Green Hills

Nashville, Tennessee United States

Gross size of center:
634,316 sq. ft.

Amount of space added or renovated:
130,000 sq. ft.

Gross leasable area excluding anchors:
300,000 sq. ft.

Total acreage of site:
26 acres

Type of center:
Regional center

Physical description:
Enclosed mall

Location of trading area:
Urban but not downtown

Population:
- Primary trading area
  355,460
- Secondary trading area
  342,958

Development schedule:
- Original opening date
  Summer 1955
- Current expansion date
  August 1993

Parking spaces:
- Present number
  2,868

Greenery and large expanses of windows give an atrium look to an entrance at The Mall at Green Hills.

Green Hills

Parking structures (in gray) bring shoppers into close proximity to anchor stores.

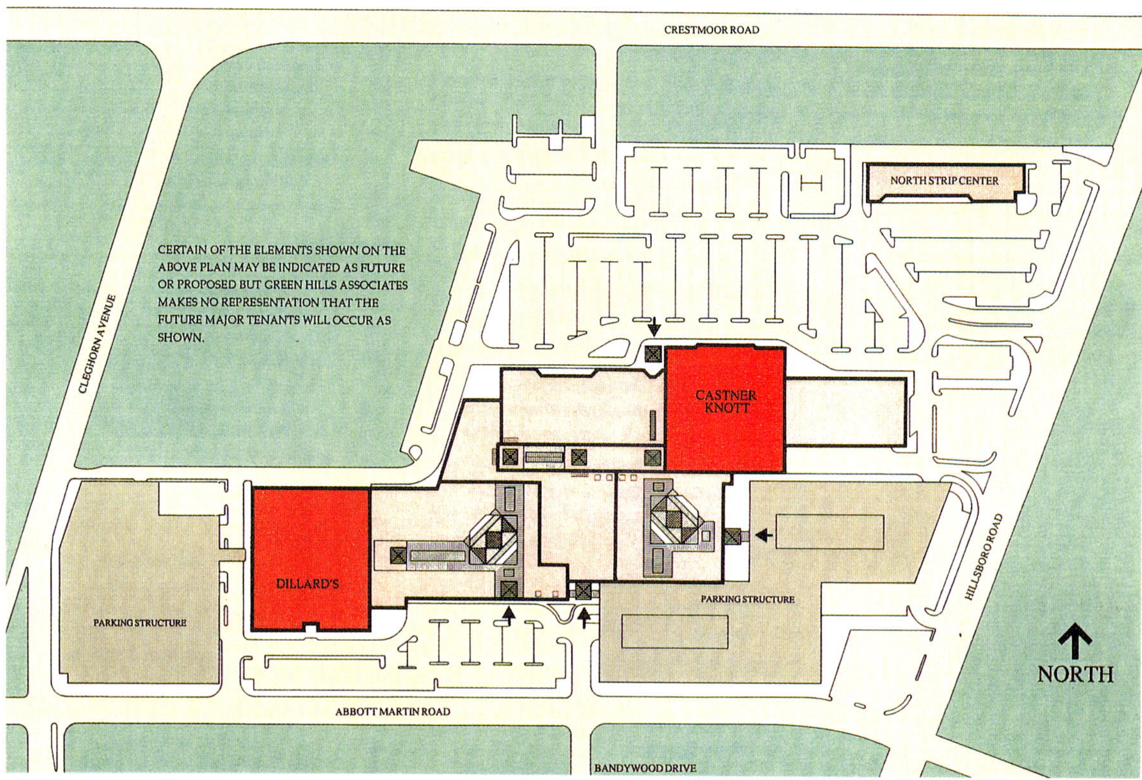

A two-level mall enclosed what had been a strip center.

Originally, the shopping center on the site of The Mall at Green Hills was a strip center. Several additions culminated in the combining of a freestanding department store, an open-air fashion strip and two single-level enclosed malls connected by escalator from a lower to a higher terrace. Each addition, however, only appeared to be another appendage, and as a result the center could not accommodate the full merchandising mix of a regional mall.

The few national stores did well. The physical condition of the center was good, the site well maintained, and the landscaping appealing. Importantly, its location in a high-income section of Nashville boded well for redevelopment possibilities.

Today, The Mall at Green Hills is a single homogeneous, enclosed two-level regional mall serving southern Nashville. Redevelopment involved creating the two-level mall itself, adding 130,000 sq. ft. of mall shops, expanding the Dillard's department store, connecting the two department stores to the mall and adding two weather-protected parking structures.

Emphasizing the Area's Roots

Design of the resulting building drew heavily on the historic and architectural roots of Tennessee in general and Nashville in particular. Both the deep red color of the native brick and the forest green trim of the door, window and skylight mullions recall the historic architecture in the adjoining countryside. Architectural forms are respectful of the original buildings' entry canopies and skylights — and in many cases these remain, thus bringing an image of permanence even after renovation, as well as a sense of commitment to the community.

By contrast, the interiors feature a clean, crisp and elegant look. A sophisticated design was applied to theatrical cornices, specialty lighting and project and tenant signage.

A dated exterior (above) gets a sharp-looking overhaul (left).

The Renovation Process

Stores were kept open throughout the renovation process, which was done in phases. Some tenants were temporarily relocated. Some pedestrian tunnels through the construction areas were created. Department stores were kept open throughout, even while Dillard's expanded its store size by one-third.

A special advertising campaign and site signage encouraged customers to shop during the construction months. Although tenants generally retained a fair sales volume, owners made concessions where required. Tenants received advance word of any construction activity that would affect their space.

The view toward the Castner-Knott anchor was transformed from low and drab to tall and airy.

New interior landscaping makes a stronger impression than the old shrubbery on an approach to the Dillard's anchor.

Even directional signage shows imagination and style.

MAJOR TENANTS		
NAME	**TYPE**	**GLA (SQ. FT.)**
Dillard's	Department store	177,000
Castner-Knott	Mercantile	133,422
Gus Mayer	Department store	19,377

The skylights provide warm natural light and architectural drama as well.

Improving Merchandise Mix

The physical changes to the center created a better ambience, but perhaps even more important was the substantial improvement in the merchandising mix brought about by attracting more prominent tenants to the center. This was accomplished through renovation and a strong marketing campaign to promote The Mall at Green Hills as the fashion leader in the region.

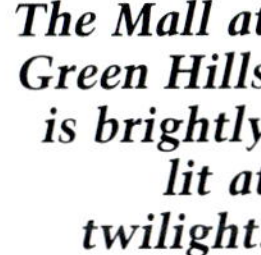

The Mall at Green Hills is brightly lit at twilight.

Renovation or Expansion of an Existing Project

Owner:
King of Prussia Associates
King of Prussia, Pennsylvania

Architect:
Thompson, Ventulett, Stainback & Associates, Inc.
Atlanta, Georgia

Designer:
W. Mark Carter
Atlanta, Georgia

Design Award

The Plaza at King of Prussia

King of Prussia, Pennsylvania United States

Gross size of center:
1,526,593 sq.ft.

Amount of space added or renovated:
268,000 sq. ft.

Gross leasable area excluding anchors:
687,004 sq. ft., including outparcels

Total acreage of site:
93 acres

Type of center:
Superregional center

Physical description:
Enclosed two-level mall

Location of trading area:
Urban to rural

Population:
- Primary trading area
  1,493,342
- Secondary trading area
  573,977

Development schedule:
- Original opening date
  September 1959
- Current expansion date
  November 1993
- Future expansion:

  Anticipated date
  November 1995

  GLA to be added
  798,607 sq. ft.

Parking spaces:
- Present number
  6,711

The renovation of The Plaza at King of Prussia introduced a classical image in center court.

REMING

The Plaza at King of Prussia opened in 1959 as a small open-air shopping center with a 35,000 sq. ft. supermarket and a few sidewalk-oriented stores. Many additions later, following the center's enclosure in the early 1980s and the opening of The Court at King of Prussia 500 feet away, the center had grown to 1,526,593 sq. ft.

Several factors added up to the redevelopment of the Plaza. First, retenanting of the Court completed in 1992 revealed that it had failed to attract new large-format specialty stores because no appropriate-size space could be found. Second, the physical appearance of the Plaza was dated. Third, some stores — particularly the supermarket still on site from the early days — needed to be removed to benefit the tenant mix. Fourth, the heating, ventilation and air conditioning (HVAC) system needed replacing. Fifth, more parking was needed.

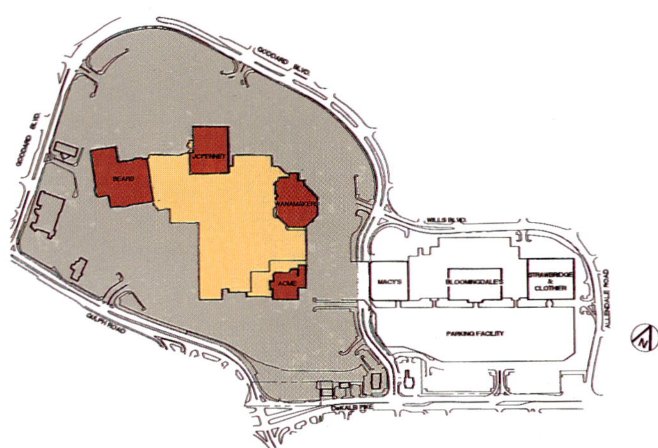

A site plan shows the proximity of The Plaza at King of Prussia (shaded area) to its sister center, The Court at King of Prussia, 500 feet away.

Photo courtesy Lawrence S. Williams, Inc.

Interior features in the two-level enclosed mall.

MAJOR TENANTS		
NAME	**TYPE**	**GLA (SQ. FT.)**
Sears	Department store	222,412
John Wanamaker	Department store	193,500
JC Penney	Department store	171,558

Finally, the Plaza itself needed to be retenanted — it was a confusing conglomeration of store types. Out-of-date local operations were present, as were stores better suited to strip centers. Popularly priced women's ready-to-wear was underrepresented as a category. A former Stern's department store had been vacant since 1986.

Five Years in the Remaking

Redevelopment was divided into four phases, stretching over five years.

Phase One, in 1988, saw the enclosure of a stream on the property to permit eventual expansion of the parking lot. Phase Two, in 1992, called for JC Penney, an anchor, to be relocated — downsized and remerchandised — into the renovated Stern's space.

Bold ceiling patterning and an embossed frieze cap the renovated court outside Wanamaker's.

Photo courtesy Brian Gassel/TVS & Associates

Photo courtesy Lawrence S. Williams, Inc.

JC Penney's move from an interior to an exterior location gave extra visibility to the store, which boosted sales.

Phases Three and Four occurred simultaneously (and began in January 1993, at the start of the worst winter ever in the area). In Phase Three, the former JC Penney space was subdivided to give the new large-format specialty stores appropriate space. Some stores, including the supermarket, were relocated to a new strip center built one mile away expressly for that purpose. In all, 20 tenants were terminated and 50 more were relocated. Phase Four saw the creation of 600 linear feet of new mall common area and the renovation of 2,560 linear feet of existing mall common area. A new central HVAC system was installed. Electrical, telephone and life-safety systems and features for persons with disabilities were upgraded to state-of-the-art systems.

Natural light and the color contrasts of building materials present an elegant fashion image for The Plaza.

Photo courtesy Brian Gassel/TVS & Associates

Extensive new skylights brightened the mall.

Glass chandeliers and coffered ceilings accompany shoppers as they travel through the mall.

Ornamental detail and grillwork accent the new plaza and draw from the area's colonial heritage.

Formal topiary dwarfs a curved bench at a center court column.

Photo courtesy Brian Gassel/TVS & Associates

Sales During Construction

Previous renovation projects had resulted in drastically decreased sales during the construction period. Special steps were taken to change that pattern. Lighthearted graphics on 1,800 feet of barricades in construction areas, as well as ports for "sidewalk superintendents," made the renovation its own attraction. Discount coupons were mailed frequently to customers, and special events were held each Thursday night, in a successful effort to sustain sales.

More Renovation to Come

The owner sought even more extensive renovation during Phases Five and Six, which were to take place the following year; therefore, Phases One through Four of the renovation were designed to make the popularly priced sections the most attractive in the entire shopping complex. These steps sustained sales during Phases Five and Six of the renovation, which were devoted to areas with the most upscale stores.

Interiors were completely reworked. Extensive new skylights brightened the new mall and courts. Patterned Italian marble floors, topiary bushes and seating areas created a European-style streetscape.

Whole-year sales in the renovation area during Phases Three and Four actually increased over the previous year and paved the way for the potential success of the even larger renovation to come.

Renovation or Expansion of an Existing Project

Owner:
The Crosland Group
Charlotte, North Carolina

Architect:
Little & Associates Architects
Charlotte, North Carolina

Designer:
Little & Associates Architects
Charlotte, North Carolina

Design Award

Sharon Corners Shopping Center

Charlotte, North Carolina United States

Gross size of center:
95,347 sq. ft.

Amount of space added or renovated:
95,347 sq. ft.

Gross leasable area excluding anchors:
95,347 sq. ft.

Total acreage of site:
10 acres

Type of center:
Neighborhood/community center

Physical description:
Strip center

Location of trading area:
Urban but not downtown

Population:
- Primary trading area
  180,000
- Secondary trading area
  350,000

Development schedule:
- Original opening date
  1962
- Current expansion date
  September 1993

Parking spaces:
- Present number
  385

Architecturally prominent features, such as the gold-topped tower, provide visual termination points and a stronger sense of place.

BELL ATLANTIC
MOBILE

An obviously aging center, some of whose key tenants were relocating to nearby sites, Sharon Corners needed to reestablish its role as a thriving, community-oriented place of business. Over the years, expansions had resulted in an inconsistent visual image and a layout that did not lend itself to strong leasing.

The center is located across from SouthPark Regional Mall at one of the most densely traveled intersections in the region and in a relatively high-income area. While optimally located, the center suffered from poor visibility because of several small outparcels. Existing tenants included a drugstore, a grocery store, a bicycle shop, a dry cleaner, a convenience store, a delicatessen and other neighborhood service operations.

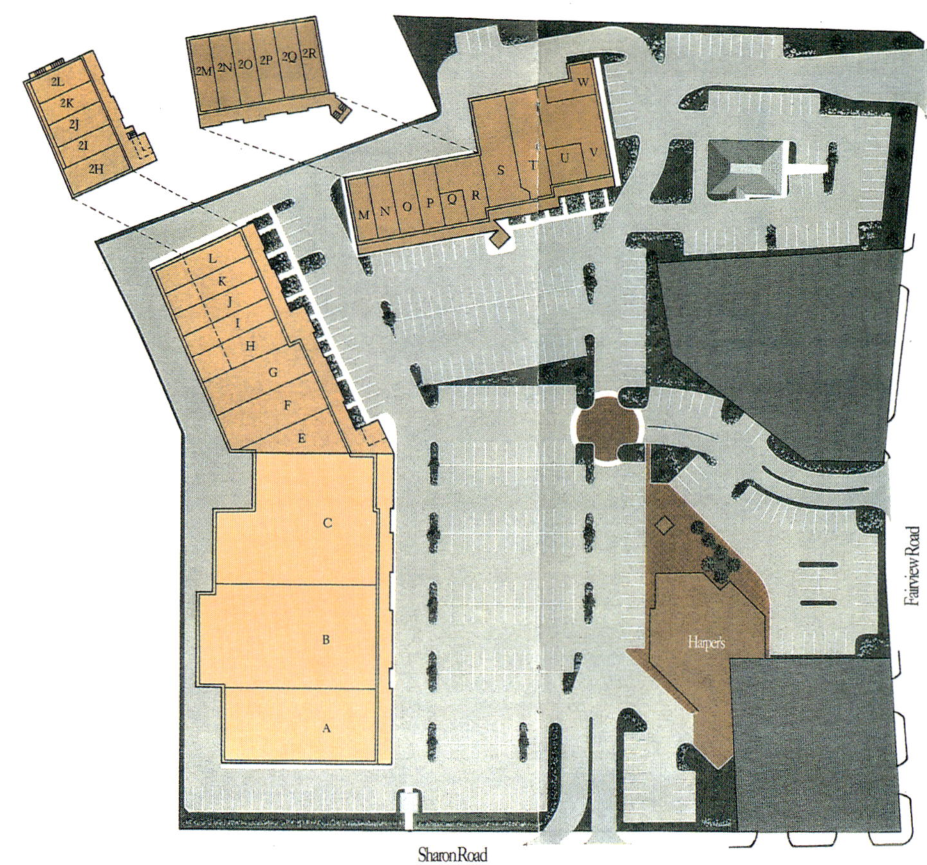

Good site utilization at Sharon Corners keeps parking spaces close to stores.

An aerial view shows the close proximity of Sharon Corners to SouthPark Regional Mall.

Photo courtesy © Carolina Photo Group

The old shopping center — plagued by an inconsistent visual image and low visibility for storefronts.

Although occupancy was high, the center's tenants did not reflect the strengths of the surrounding business market, and many tenants' length of stay was evident in rents that were low for the region. The grocery store was planning a relocation, and a library previously on the site had already relocated. The owner decided the time was ripe for change.

MAJOR TENANTS		
NAME	TYPE	GLA (SQ. FT.)
Barnes & Noble	Bookstore	14,764
Men's Warehouse	Apparel	13,716
Eckerd Drugs	Drugstore	8,775
Jesse Brown's Outfitters	Apparel	7,200

Creating Visual Closure

The redesign of the center rested on two key concepts: forming a visual closure around the existing parking lot to achieve a sense of exterior space and creating specific axes of vision with architecturally prominent terminations to provide a stronger sense of place.

A Warm Ambiance

Details and materials used in construction were chosen to convey the traditions of southeast Charlotte without duplicating colonial details. A special run of Phoenix-tumbled brick included the irregular texture and soft edges typically found on handmade brick. A light silica sand applied to the face gives the exterior the warm ambience of century-old buildings.

Charlotte's colonial heritage influences the look of even a Chinese restaurant.

The center's exterior recreates the warm ambiance of century-old buildings.

Photo courtesy Rick Alexander & Associates. © 1993.

Tenant and Shopper Needs

The center was operational throughout the four phases of construction. Tenants that chose to remain in the center after renovation were relocated into existing vacant space not affected by the current phase of construction. When the first phase was completed, those tenants were moved again into newly renovated space. Shopper safety was maintained by fencing off construction areas.

More New Efforts

Marketing components of the renovation included changing the name of the center to Sharon Corners, introducing a new logo, flying seasonal banners and vastly improving marketing and leasing print materials.

Although the new visual image of the renovated Sharon Corners is decidedly that of an upscale strip center, leasing plans went beyond high-end retailers. An effective mix of merchants and restaurants gives the center a neighborhood feel appropriate to an upscale community.

A special run of Phoenix-tumbled brick lent warmth to the overall look of Sharon Corners.

Roof heights were varied to give individual identity to retailers.

Photo courtesy Rick Alexander & Associates. © 1993.

Renovation or Expansion of an Existing Project

Owner:
The Prudential Insurance Company of America
Newark, New Jersey

Architect:
Sikes, Jennings, Kelly & Brewer
Houston, Texas

Designer:
Communication Arts
Boulder, Colorado

Design Award

The Shops at Prudential Center

Boston, Massachusetts United States

Gross size of center:
492,826 sq. ft.

Amount of space added or renovated:
140,000 sq. ft.

Gross leasable area excluding anchors:
252,923 sq. ft.

Total acreage of site:
26 acres

Type of center:
Multi-use center

Physical description:
Enclosed one-level mall

Location of trading area:
Urban central business district

Population:
- Primary trading area
  600,000
- Secondary trading area
  5,600,000

Development schedule:
- Original opening date
  April 19, 1965
- Current expansion date
  October 15, 1993

Parking spaces:
- Present number
  3,100

Climate-controlled arcades demonstrate how Prudential Center has become a shopper-friendly environment.

FIRST ISSUE
Kids

Prudential Center before (above) and after the renovation (left).

The site plan shows how The Shops at Prudential Center (brown) wrap around office, retail and convention space.

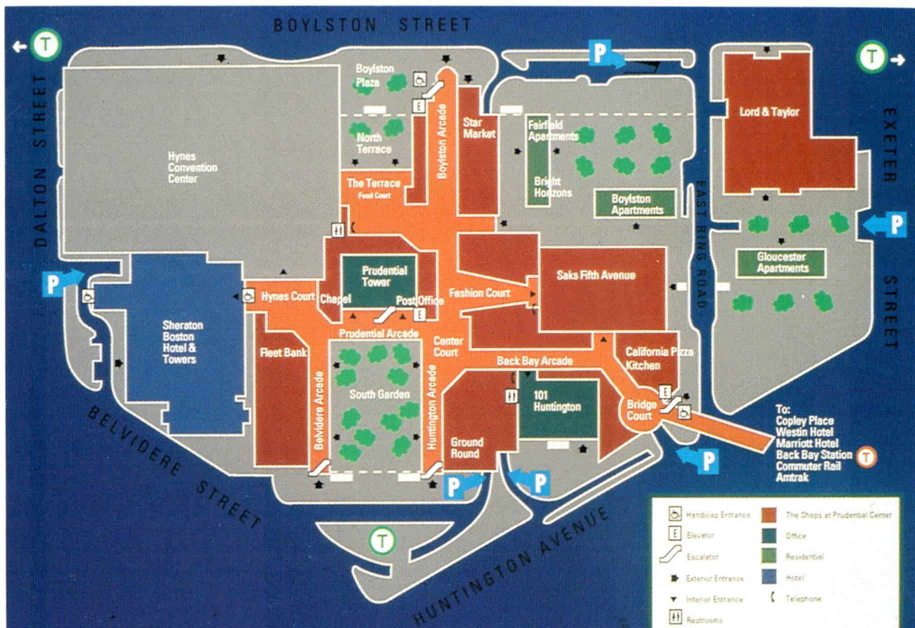

Prudential Center opened in 1965 as a mixed-use real estate development, containing 500,000 sq. ft. of retail, 1.8 million sq. ft. of office, Boston's largest hotel, 800 luxury apartments and a 3,100-car garage.

Designed in the late 1950s, the single-sided retail component of Prudential Center had physical difficulties for retailers. Built over the Massachusetts Turnpike and railroad lines, shopping concourses had to be constructed 22 feet above sidewalk level, thereby disconnecting the retail from the surrounding neighborhoods. Retail arcades were enclosed but not climate controlled. The anchor tenants, Saks Fifth Avenue and Lord & Taylor, were not physically connected and were accessible only via windswept plazas.

The center's look had become outdated by the mid-1980s when Boston's Back Bay area retail was revitalized by the construction of the upscale Copley Place mall and the rebirth of shops and galleries adjacent to Prudential Center. Simultaneously the city's convention center, to the west of Prudential Center, was expanded. These developments increased the flow of pedestrian traffic through Prudential Center to roughly 30,000 per day, but sales at the stores in the center continued to fall.

Redevelopment turned a barren outdoor plaza (above) into a lively gathering place (below).

MAJOR TENANTS

NAME	TYPE	GLA (SQ. FT.)
Lord & Taylor	Department store	129,300
Saks Fifth Avenue	Department store	110,603
Star Market	Supermarket	35,000

Drawing Shoppers

The Prudential undertook a redevelopment effort that made The Shops at Prudential Center a shopping destination for office workers, hotel guests, conventioneers and others. The renovation changed the one-sided retail configuration into a double-sided, glass-enclosed, climate-controlled shopping environment. Saks Fifth Avenue was renovated and connected directly to the retail concourses. A new enclosed link from Copley Place to Prudential Center draws guests from Copley's two convention hotels as well as commuters using the Back Bay train station. Entrances were redesigned to welcome shoppers approaching from street level.

The Construction Phase

Only five retailers — a bank, a restaurant, two sandwich shops and a card shop — remained open during construction, to serve office workers. Nevertheless, safe pedestrian access was needed for the thousands of people who crossed the site each day. Covered walkways were created, with upbeat graphics and printed maps to help pedestrians find their way and learn what was open or closed during renovation. Monthly redevelopment newsletters updated office and residential tenants. A construction hotline was installed.

The plaza at the north side of Prudential Tower (right) was enclosed to create a food court (above).

Saks Fifth Avenue gained a light and bright renovated entrance.

Mall Enhancements

The 3,100-car garage was enhanced with new paint and lighting as well as a comprehensive signage package for directions and information. Expanded vertical access points made it easier to get into and out of retail arcades. Parking validation was established to draw suburbanites to shop at the center. State-of-the-art security was brought in along with automated building controls. Outdoor spaces were enhanced with seating and new landscaping.

The store mix was revitalized as well and sought to complement the area's existing retail. The variety of shops and restaurants meets the needs of Prudential Center's 4,000 office workers, 1,200 apartment tenants and 51,000 residents of nearby neighborhoods and includes a supermarket, a housewares store, a post office, a chapel, a bookstore, apparel and specialty shops and a range of restaurants and take-out food outlets.

New extended shopping hours proved an important advantage to The Shops at Prudential Center's retailers. Strict guidelines for store-front design and close management of buildout gave an interesting streetlike flavor to the retail arcades. A cross-media advertising and promotional campaign told potential shoppers that "The heart of Boston now has a soul."

Renovation Benefits

Occupancy rates of office and retail space, as well as retail sales, have benefited substantially from the renovation, which was recognized by the Boston Redevelopment Authority and others as an innovative model for mitigating the negative impact of development. Working around the constraints of existing structures and its location over a highway, the renovation has bolstered the performance of all components in the mixed-use complex and energized a languishing section of the city.

Views of the arcades.

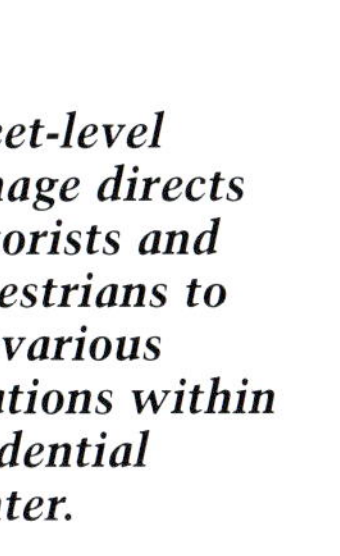

Street-level signage directs motorists and pedestrians to the various locations within Prudential Center.

Renovation or Expansion of an Existing Project

Owner:
Downtown Plaza Associates
San Diego, California

Architect:
The Jerde Partnership
Venice, California

Designer:
The Jerde Partnership
Venice, California

Certificate of Merit

Downtown Plaza

Sacramento, California United States

Gross size of center:
927,000 sq. ft.

Amount of space added or renovated:
166,500 sq. ft.

Gross leasable area excluding anchors:
358,500 sq. ft.

Type of center:
Regional multi-use center

Physical description:
Open two-level mall

Location of trading area:
Urban central business district

Population:
- Primary trading area
  1,162,204
- Secondary trading area
  1,663,274

Development schedule:
- Original opening date
  September 1971
- Current expansion date
  October 1993

Parking spaces:
- Present number
  4,000

Over one million dollars in fine art was placed throughout Downtown Plaza.

G
A
KEEPER
MASTERMIND

Sacramento, whose population growth rate almost doubled that of the nation during the 1980s, had become understored by the end of the decade. City government targeted its central business district for a major revitalization to include new hotels, office towers, shops, services and recreation facilities.

Downtown Plaza, a 1971 single-level retail and office complex in the central business district, was in need of revitalization as well. Vacancy was relatively low, but so were sales. Its architecture was staid and uninviting, its signage almost nonexistent and its tenant mix unexciting. A 120-foot-wide main mall — actually a blocked-off city street — discouraged cross-shopping.

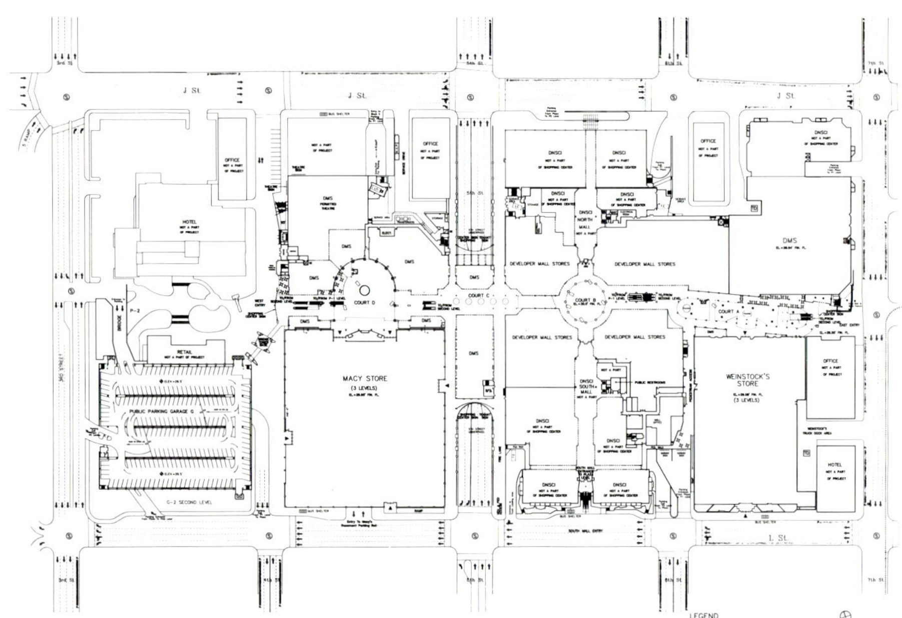

The site plan and an aerial view show Downtown Plaza nestled in the central business district of Sacramento.

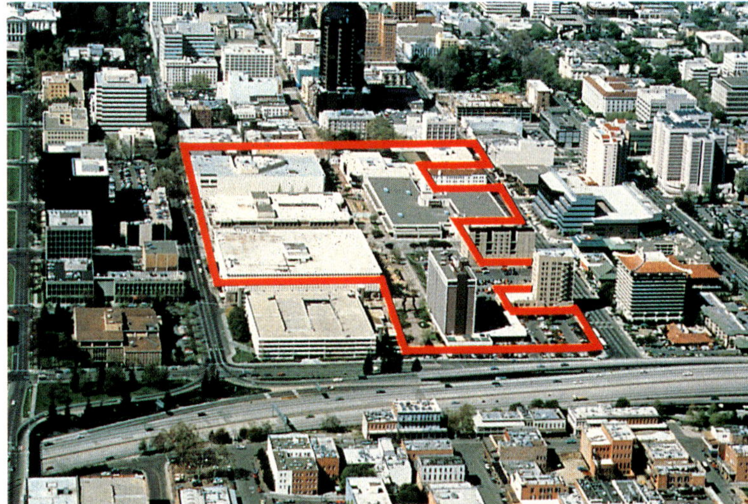

Downtown Plaza had an old (below left) and a new way (below right) to design around a vehicular tunnel.

MAJOR TENANTS		
NAME	**TYPE**	**GLA (SQ. FT.)**
Macy's	Department store	332,500
Weinstocks	Department store	171,000
America Live!	Dining/entertainment complex	65,000

Each of the center's four courts assumed a separate identity.

Downtown Plaza needed more than a paint job, the owner decided. Instead, plans were made to reinvent Downtown Plaza with a more inviting atmosphere, a wider retail selection and more dining and entertainment options.

Downtown Plaza was recreated as a series of four courts (the architect calls them "urban rooms"): an Old World marketplace, an intimate London street, a formal Italian garden and a court with classic American elegance. Arcades connect the courts. Although the center remains open-air, awnings and overhangs offer customers protection from too much sun or inclement weather. Mall width now averages 30 feet, making cross-shopping easier.

New Built Atop Old

The architect and designer sought to retain a sense of history while establishing a new look. The result is a layering effect that gives many the impression that the center grew over time as Sacramento did, with new built on top of old. As one views the project from the ground skyward, massive stone masonry transitions into light modern forms of steel and metal.

The center's palette features earthy hues of terra cotta and muted shades of blue and olive, accented with teak and polished metals. Dramatic lighting and laser displays lend ambiance and high-tech excitement. To climax the center's visual appeal, $1.2 million worth of original fine-art pieces and foundations of hand-crafted tiles are found throughout the complex.

Entertainment Focus

Both ends of Downtown Plaza focus on entertainment. At the west entrance is The Piazza, whose upper level houses a multi-screen cinema and a food court. The Piazza's lower level features whimsical retailing — a Warner Bros. Studio Store and The Great Train Store — as well as a two-story microbrewery. At the opposite end

Within the center, oversized cartoon stars attract shoppers to a Warner Bros. Studio Store.

Massive stone masonry transitions into light, modern forms of steel and metal.

of the center, adjacent to the major downtown terminus of the light rail system, is America Live!, a 64,000 sq. ft. multi-venued dining and entertainment complex. America Live! replaced an I. Magnin store, whose closing caused a major re-leasing challenge and a temporary halt to construction.

Talking to Shoppers

Shoppers' curiosity was encouraged and satisfied throughout the renovation process. Interactive barricade panels were placed in high-traffic corners. The panels featured photographic enlargements and 90-second audio recordings of people involved in the project, from the architect to the mayor. Customers could pick up a panel-mounted telephone to hear information, updated bi-weekly, about the project. Print advertising featured retailers and others involved in the renovation.

The public's appetite was further whetted by featuring the actual finish materials on panels near where the four courts were being built. A customer newsletter was distributed on-site and to area office buildings. A "Van About Town" began to provide free giftwrap and delivery service within a specified radius. Finally, the grand opening promotion featured a remake of Petula Clark's pop classic song, "Downtown." As a result of these marketing efforts, 98 percent of invited retailers remained in the project during construction. Some saw increased sales during the renovation period.

Success' Ripple Effect

Beyond its own success, the redevelopment of Downtown Plaza is having a ripple effect throughout the central business district. Retail vacancy on adjacent streets has dropped dramatically. Even the competing "Old Sacramento" historic retail district is posting sales gains from shopper overflow and cross-shopping. Further development of the area will include expansion of the convention center, a federal courthouse, other government construction, 8,000,000 sq. ft. of offices and homes for 2,400 residents. City officials agree that Downtown Plaza itself has become an anchor for the west end of downtown Sacramento.

Laser displays energize a concert at the main court.

The closing of the I. Magnin anchor (above left) presented a challenge met by the America Live! entertainment center (left).

Renovation or Expansion of an Existing Project

Owner:
Equitable Real Estate Investment Management, Inc.
Atlanta, Georgia

Architect:
Shapiro Petrauskas Gelber
Philadelphia, Pennsylvania

Certificate of Merit

Granite Run Mall

Media, Pennsylvania
United States

Gross size of center:
1,041,572 sq. ft.

Amount of space added or renovated:
90,000 sq. ft.

Gross leasable area excluding anchors:
317,703 sq. ft.

Total acreage of site:
85.4 acres

Type of center:
Regional center

Physical description:
Enclosed two-level mall

Location of trading area:
Suburban

Population:
- Primary trading area
  496,000
- Secondary trading area
  180,000

Development schedule:
- Original opening date
  Fall 1973
- Current expansion date
  November 1993
- Future expansion:

  GLA to be added
  150,000 sq. ft.

Parking spaces:
- Present number
  5,100

The entrances to Granite Run Mall were built up and lightened, giving them greater visibility from the parking lots.

Five years of declining traffic, sales, market share, occupancy and net operating income led the owner of Granite Run Mall to undertake a renovation and re-leasing program.

The challenges were many. The 20-year-old mall was in an extremely competitive and overbuilt retail market. The mall's physical appearance and tenant mix were dated, and an anchor store space was vacant. Storefront visibility between the two levels and at courts was virtually nonexistent. Inadequate vertical circulation meant one entire leg of the mall towards JC Penney had no traffic. Promotional activities and temporary tenant programs were precluded by the limitations of the facility. Even mall entries were nearly unidentifiable from the parking lots.

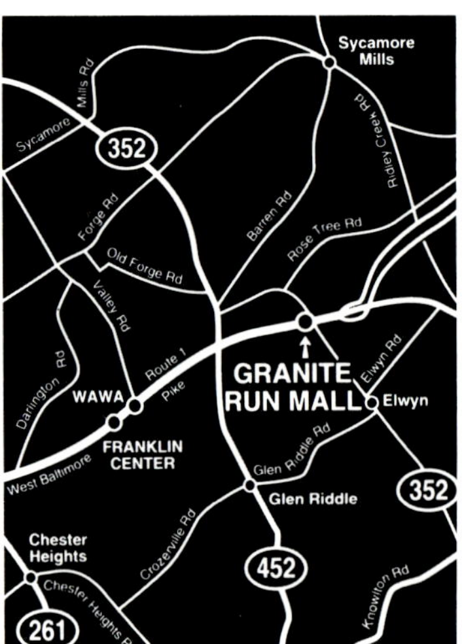

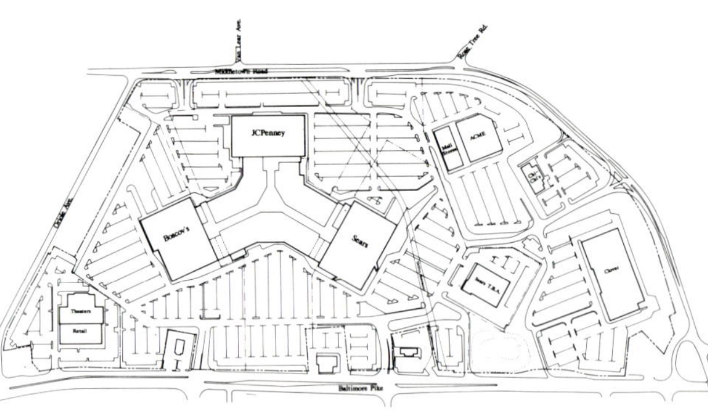

Granite Run Mall has a triangular layout, as shown in the site plan and aerial view.

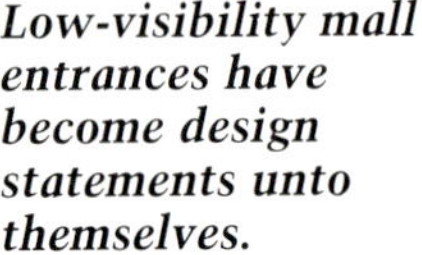

Low-visibility mall entrances have become design statements unto themselves.

Atop the renovation's priority list were merchant visibility and access. Larger and simplified well openings were designed, especially at courts, to open up sightlines to storefronts. New escalators were installed to bring traffic into the JC Penney wing. Renovation permitted the introduction of kiosk and pushcart programs. In addition, a major public space was created by eliminating pools, bridges and landings at the center court.

Renovation plans attracted tenants that had previously turned down a location at Granite Run, as well as a new anchor, Boscov's, to fill the vacant anchor space. Key mall tenants were split between floors: The Gap, The Bombay Company and Natural Wonders on the upper floor, with The Disney Store, Lerner New York and Merry Go Round on the lower level. This effort changed old traffic patterns, and customer movement between floors is now well balanced.

The new anchor, Boscov's, has a strong presence at both mall levels.

MAJOR TENANTS

NAME	TYPE	GLA (SQ. FT.)
Sears	Department store	175,300
Boscov's	Department store	174,717
JC Penney	Department store	150,792
Clover	Freestand	82,500
Acme Food Market & Shops	Supermarket	55,236

Granite Run Mall's pylon and marquee introduce the clean bright lines of the renovation.

Pre- (below) and post- (above) renovation photographs bring Granite Run Mall from the 1970s into the 1990s.

Exploring the New Stores

Retailers benefited from the center's award-winning marketing program "Perks with Purchase," which gives customers incentives to try new stores on each shopping visit. The program also provides new names for the center's mailing list database.

The entire center, except for the new Boscov's, was open during renovation, and all stores were accessible. The center court was temporarily enclosed, but "show windows" satisfied shoppers' curiosity. Security tunnels were built at entries. As a cost-saver, much of the demolition and construction was done during shopping hours; extra mall maintenance and security patrols helped ensure cleanliness and safety. Mall management used weekly personal visits and newsletters to keep tenants aware of renovation progress.

Interior and Exterior Changes

Outside, mall entries were built up and lightened, giving them greater visibility from parking lots. The entire site was studied for new efficiencies in traffic flow and parking. Traffic was rerouted, signals adjusted, signage added and approximately 55 new parking spaces added.

On the inside, visual change was created in cost-effective ways. For example, most flooring is inexpensive porcelain tile, but an impression of richness is left by the marble used in the courts and at column bases. The designer avoided presenting a too-upscale image that would clash with the pricepoints of existing retailers.

Demand for Space

Retailers' enthusiasm for the redevelopment is reflected in the 35 percent of GLA leased to tenants new to the center's market. In addition, the new stores are creating demand for the remaining space at Granite Run Mall.

Flooring tile and column bases demonstrate how design accents were focused at the courts.

Escalators and towers soar above shoppers.

Renovation or Expansion of an Existing Project

Owner:
Property Capital Trust
Boston, Massachusetts

Architect:
John R. DeBello, Architect
Deerfield Beach, Florida

Designer:
SullivanPerkins
Dallas, Texas

Certificate of Merit

Loehmann's Fashion Island

Aventura, Florida
United States

Gross size of center:
279,983 sq. ft.

Amount of space added or renovated:
279,878 sq. ft.

Gross leasable area excluding anchors:
279,878 sq. ft.

Total acreage of site:
27.46 acres

Type of center:
Fashion/specialty neighborhood center

Physical description:
One-level open mall

Location of trading area:
Urban but not downtown

Population:
- Primary trading area
  101,238
- Secondary trading area
  431,253

Development schedule:
- Original opening date
  December 1, 1980
- Current expansion date
  December 5, 1993

Parking spaces:
- Present number
  1,572
- 500 parking spaces to be added

Shade structures over seating areas let in adequate amounts of Florida sunshine.

After only 13 years, the open-air Loehmann's Plaza had become a rundown center with less than one-third occupancy. It was unattractive and had a poor public image as crime-ridden and unsafe. The tenant mix consisted of Loehmann's discount fashion store and a few other retailers. There were even spaces in the center with dirt floors — they had never been leased.

Revitalizing the center into Loehmann's Fashion Island required physical, architectural and design improvements, re-leasing and marketing. From a design perspective, Loehmann's Plaza looked dull. Lighting failed to draw attention to storefronts, sides of buildings were large expanses of unbroken off-white, and walkways were dark and drab.

Occupancy at Loehmann's Fashion Island skyrocketed because of renovation plans.

An anonymous exterior project entrance (left) now says "Florida" to anyone approaching (below).

Bas-reliefs and sculptures of birds on signs, at key vistas and other locations, offer a lighthearted visual theme.

Much of the new look of Loehmann's Fashion Island comes from overhead wooden trellislike structures whose open sections and shade devices alternately admit the Florida sunshine and create a continously changing pattern of shaded areas. Landscaping now abounds. Stylish seating provides shopper comfort, and floors feature pastel tile designs. Dramatic lighting, at night now draws shoppers' attention to store windows. Bas-reliefs and sculptures of birds on signs and at key vistas within the center offer a lighthearted visual theme.

Bright signage helps shoppers find their way within the renovated center.

Adapting to Renovation

Given a horseshoe-shaped open-air center with internal traffic circulation, maintaining continuous mall operations during construction proved to be a challenge. Temporary storefronts were built three feet inside each existing tenant space so the exterior skin of the building could be demolished and replaced. At times, scaffold tunnels were erected to protect shoppers from overhead construction. At other times, small bridges were built to move patrons over exposed excavations that required several days or weeks to complete. Construction of common areas needed painted barricades to bisect the space so traffic could flow on one side while the other was under construction.

Marketing Loehmann's Fashion Island was integral to the success of the renovation. Previously, the mall had not been marketed as one entity. Marketing the new center involved advertising, entertainment, community programs and charity events. Advertising sought to attract both new customers and new retailers. A merchant productivity program based on monthly meetings, customer service evaluations and assistance in visual merchandising fostered positive relationships between owner and tenants, as well as sales increases.

MAJOR TENANTS

NAME	TYPE	GLA (SQ. FT.)
Publix	Supermarket	47,813
AMC Fashion Island 16 Theaters	Cinemas	47,220
Loehmann's	Discount fashion	19,645
Barnes & Noble	Bookstore	10,511
Jeweler's Exchange	Jewelry market	9,915

Much of the new look comes from overhead trellislike structures.

A leasing plan was developed to link the off-price Loehmann's store with traditional mall retailers and upscale regional stores that specialize in fashion, gifts, furniture and housewares.

Redevelopment and re-leasing also gave the Aventura community a focal point. Nestled between Miami and Fort Lauderdale, the sophisticated and affluent neighborhood had lacked a place of its own. Also, the center is less than one mile from hotel-dotted beaches full of foreign and domestic visitors. Restaurants, outdoor cafés, art galleries and a 16-theater complex add entertainment to the new mix, attracting area shoppers and giving the Aventura community a safe, appealing shopping destination that matches the ambience of its surroundings.

Landscaping throughout Loehmann's Fashion Island benefits from the midday sun while shoppers take advantage of the shade.

Renovation or Expansion of an Existing Project

Owner:
Westcor Partners/Corporate Property Investors (DVM Co.)
Phoenix, Arizona

Architect:
Callison Architecture, Inc.
Seattle, Washington

Designer:
Callison Architecture, Inc.
Seattle, Washington

Certificate of Merit

Metrocenter

Phoenix, Arizona
United States

Gross size of center:
1,551,240 sq. ft.

Amount of space added or renovated:
1,551,240 sq. ft.

Gross leasable area excluding anchors:
1,352,000 sq. ft.

Total acreage of site:
92 acres

Type of center:
Regional center

Physical description:
Two-level enclosed mall

Location of trading area:
N/A

Development schedule:
- Original opening date
  1973
- Current expansion date
  Fall 1993

Parking spaces:
- Present number
  7,200

Metrocenter's new design includes marble-clad columns, alabaster light fixtures and palm trees.

COUNTY·SEAT
Fitting Image

A new mall to be developed less than 10 miles away was the principal motivation behind the renovation of Metrocenter, opened in 1973 as Phoenix's first superregional center.

Metrocenter had always been a dominant leader in the Phoenix retail market, with 1.3 million sq. ft. of stores anchored by major department stores. Until 1991, the center had enjoyed little competition, although in recent years a significant number of strip and power centers had opened in the area. With the new mall to open soon, Metrocenter's owner took a proactive stance and began requiring renovation from tenants whose leases expired in 1992. More than 60 stores were remodeled in just one year. The next step was to bring the mall's aesthetics up to par with the new store formats.

Skylights in the scalloped ceiling (above) were enlarged to admit natural light (below).

Photo courtesy A.F. Payne Photographic. © 1993.

A court's sculpture was replaced by high-flying water sprays.

The mall's old appearance made some strong statements. Ceilings were sculpted in a large-scale scalloped design. In some areas, low-lying drywall "clouds" reduced the amount of light and made spaces seem smaller. The floor surface was a dark tile that weighed down the interior's look. The signage, graphics and overall identity of the mall were outdated and no longer represented the tenant mix.

The goal of renovation was to create a visual identity that would carry Metrocenter into the 21st century. Design would focus on the Southwestern locale and high-desert environment of the valley surrounding Metrocenter.

MAJOR TENANTS

NAME	TYPE	GLA (SQ. FT.)
Dillard's	Department store	N/A
The Broadway	Department store	N/A
Robinson's	Department store	N/A
Sears	Department store	N/A

Tapping Native Design

Overall, the design is modeled after Native American geometric patterns and serves to direct shoppers to the center court, which is highlighed by marble-clad columns, alabaster light fixtures and palm trees. The new flooring is a stone field accented with red, white, black and turquoise marble. At the ends of the center court, circular portals are illuminated each evening, giving the appearance of the moon over a desert floor.

High priority was placed on adding natural light. Expansive skylights of fretted glass now run the entire length of the center. The pattern was chosen to reduce heat from the sun while minimizing cooling expense.

The extras were not overlooked. Elevators were renovated, and each has a new cab encased in stone, clear glass and decorative metal; the new signature graphic (a large ribbon "M") appears across the top of each elevator. Two "performing" fountains shoot slender plumes of water from black river rock and granite. New service components include information kiosks, restaurants, a concierge desk with wheelchair and stroller rentals and family rest rooms with attractive infant care centers.

A revitalized exterior is highlighted by the red-ribbon "M" design concept that is carried through in the interior as well.

Photo courtesy A.F. Payne Photographic. © 1993.

Keeping the Customer

Recognizing the existing competition, Metrocenter's marketing team feared customers would form shopping habits elsewhere during the year-long redevelopment. A special marketing campaign drove home the message that despite the construction, Metrocenter had more selection than its competitors. Frequent shoppers were rewarded with free gifts. Areas under construction were masked with decorative and informational signage and barricade treatments. Sales did not suffer during construction.

The marketing campaign was supported by communication with tenants about the various construction phases and steps being taken to assure shopper safety. Clearly illustrated graphics were displayed on barricades, giving shoppers instructions about directions and obstacles to avoid. Large portable dust covers were draped over tenant entrances every evening. Each morning began with a full mall cleanup.

Timing the Grand Reopening

The owner's only "second thought" was about timing, since Metrocenter's grand reopening was the same week as that of the new competing mall, and there might have been an advantage in building in six months' lead time to establish Metrocenter's new identity. Nonetheless, both shoppers and tenants like the revitalized center. Traffic counts have increased, customers are staying longer, tenants are committing to investing in their stores' renovation and new retailers are seeking opportunities to lease space in Metrocenter.

A new directory (right) and highly visible customer service desk (below) make Metrocenter user-friendly.

Renovation or Expansion of an Existing Project

Certificate of Merit

MicMac Mall

Dartmouth, Nova Scotia Canada

Owner:
Markborough Properties
Toronto, Ontario
Canada

Architect:
Lydon Lynch Architects
Halifax, Nova Scotia
Canada

Designer:
Maria Manoliu and Associates Limited
Toronto, Ontario
Canada

Gross size of center:
543,498 sq. ft.

Amount of space added or renovated:
102,698 sq. ft.

Gross leasable area excluding anchors:
287,546 sq. ft.

Total acreage of site:
54 acres

Type of center:
Regional fashion center

Physical description:
Enclosed three-level mall

Location of trading area:
Suburban

Population:
- Primary trading area 104,066
- Secondary trading area 314,449

Development schedule:
- Original opening date October 1973
- Current expansion date October 1993
- Future expansion:

  Anticipated date October 1995

  GLA to be added 80,000 sq. ft.

Parking spaces:
- Present number 3,001

New skylights, escalators and ceilings were added to the renovated MicMac Mall.

LOTTERY

Bright banners, natural lighting and tall plantings draw shoppers' attention overhead.

MicMac Mall is a three-level regional mall located on two of the busiest arterials in the Halifax/Dartmouth, Nova Scotia basin. The mall opened in 1973 and, by 1992, found itself rapidly losing its customer base to newly renovated centers in the competing Halifax market. Much of the third floor was vacant, and the mall's sales performance had deteriorated to the point that one viable option was to abandon the third floor altogether.

The chosen alternative, however, was to reposition the center with modern design, shopper amenities and a better tenant mix. Plans for renovation included third-floor reconstruction to straighten angular walls, thus improving the visibility of merchants and correcting both too-deep and too-shallow retail units. New skylights, escalators and ceilings would be added, as well as marble flooring, landscaped courts, directories and a central courtyard containing 50-foot palms and a fountain. A new food court would be designed. A large suspended clock, colorful banners and an identity program of new graphics and signage completed the transformation.

Food court graphics and banners create a festive ambience for eating.

MicMac's owner also knew that the store mix needed to be updated, particularly in its fashion tenants, to attract the younger and more affluent shoppers who were frequenting other centers. Redevelopment plans brought in new high-visibility retailers, including Toys 'R' Us, The Gap, The Disney Store, Eddie Bauer and Club Monaco. Many national and U.S. retailers brought their 1990s prototype stores to MicMac, in many cases the first and only such store east of Montreal. Virtually every tenant that remained undertook significant storefront renovation. The leases of tenants not matching the new mix were either not renewed or bought out.

"If It's On Your Mind..."

Renovating and remerchandising the mall involved developing a "spokescharacter" to add a humorous touch to communicating construction progress. Newspaper ads, billboards and direct-mail pieces announced the arrival of new tenants and reported on construction. Programs were adapted to reach out to distinct ethnic groups in the market. MicMac also created a new positioning statement: "If It's On Your Mind, It's In Our Mall." The grand reopening served as a fund-raiser for the Nova Scotia Special Olympics.

A literal rendition of MicMac Mall's new theme, "If it's on your mind, it's in our mall."

Younger and more affluent shoppers are now attracted to MicMac for its high-visibility retailers, such as Toys 'R' Us.

MAJOR TENANTS

NAME	TYPE	GLA (SQ. FT.)
The Bay	Department store	151,303
Eaton's	Department store	79,149
Toys 'R' Us	Toy store	30,000
IGA	Supermarket	25,500
The Gap	Apparel	14,000

Construction Coordination

MicMac Mall was kept open during construction with no loss in retail sales, and a full-time on-site tenant coordinator assisted tenants with their renovation as well as working as a liaison between tenants and the general contractor. Asbestos removal and overhead demolition were done at night. MicMac used standards of air monitoring and safety exceeding those of the U.S. Environmental Protection Agency, which are judged to be more strict than Canadian standards. Cleanup was done each morning before the mall opened its doors. Ceiling work was done by rolling scaffold, and tile was laid by alternating sections, thus preserving daytime access to all stores.

ExteriorRenovation

Exterior renovation was limited, focusing on canopies, signage and site work, in the belief that the interior would have greater consumer impact — a decision the owner thinks might have been reconsidered. Also, the owner says, a simpler means of relocating tenants during renovation might have been developed.

Destination Center

Nevertheless, the renovation of MicMac Mall took a tired center with 1970s retail concepts and created a fully leased project with continually increasing sales performance. With many stores unique to Atlantic Canada, MicMac Mall once again claims to be the destination shopping center in the Maritimes.

Graphics played a large role in the renovation, from logo redesign to cartoonlike barricade information.

Renovation or Expansion of an Existing Project

Owner:
New England Development
Newton, Massachusetts

Architect:
Arrowstreet Inc.
Somerville, Massachusetts

Designer:
Arrowstreet Inc.
Somerville, Massachusetts

Certificate of Merit

The Northshore Mall

Peabody, Massachusetts United States

Gross size of center:
1,700,000 sq. ft.

Amount of space added or renovated:
509,009 sq. ft.

Gross leasable area excluding anchors:
505,875 sq. ft.

Total acreage of site:
108 acres

Type of center:
Regional center

Physical description:
Enclosed mall

Location of trading area:
Suburban

Population:
- Primary trading area
  151,000
- Secondary trading area
  231,000

Development schedule:
- Original opening date
  1958
- Current expansion date
  November 15, 1993

Parking spaces:
- Present number
  7,680

The Northshore Mall's new food court features festive column capitals traced in neon.
Photo courtesy Robert E. Mikrut, © 1993.

FILENE'S BASEMENT
Dot
Sale

By mid-1992 The Northshore Mall was emerging from bankruptcy with a new owner. It had become understored; its appearance was drab. The mall was losing its market to a more upscale mall 15 minutes away. Other problems were traceable to enclosing the mall 16 years earlier: the then-owner had failed to place a strong anchor at one end to draw shoppers through the mall, there was an overly wide concourse, and sidewalks in the open-air center had become merely sloping mall walkways.

Redeveloping Northshore meant getting a new tenant mix, but also making mall layout a tool for remerchandising. Changes in the tenant mix began by increasing the number of anchor tenants from three to five. Existing anchors were renovated. Filene's was rebuilt in a new location at the back of the site, previously unanchored, and paired there with a new Lord & Taylor. The mall was extended and reconfigured so the tenant spaces could be designed for today's retailers, who have very different frontage and depth requirements than did the retailers of 40 or even 20 years ago.

New leasable area was added below grade for an off-price zone, which was achieved by placing Filene's Basement and Milton's into what had been a below-grade truck tunnel.

MAJOR TENANTS

NAME	TYPE	GLA (SQ. FT.)
Lord & Taylor	Department store	120,000
Jordan Marsh	Department store	302,322
Filene's	Department store	200,000
JC Penney	Department store	138,212
Sears	Department store	223,661
The Limited	Department store	N/A
Superplex	Cinema	N/A

Northshore Mall and retailers alike enjoy high visibility at night.

The interior design concept created an upscale environment with a new look and feel. The sloping walkways were replaced by a classic tile floor pattern of white, gray and black with accents of garnet-colored granite. Storefronts were brought forward 10 feet on each side to create a brighter yet more intimate street of high-fashion shops in place of the broad, drab corridors of the old mall. Skylights with planters alternate with coffered neon-edged ceilings in the new arcade. The new food court features festive column capitals traced in neon, as well as custom-designed lamps and banners hung from structures of painted metal and natural wood.

The food court calls out to hungry shoppers by day and by night.

Computers as Planning Tools

Computer support played a key role in the redevelopment. The architect's proprietary software tied rental income stream to construction phasing, making it possible to maximize the mall's functioning during the fast-track building process. Also, a computer-drawn plan was updated continually to provide information on when and where construction would occur, on where leasing activity was happening and on the scheduling of tenant construction and openings. Using this tool, design and construction could be rescheduled to accommodate specific leases as they were negotiated, while real costs could be associated with each change to provide the owner with data on the economic impact of decisions.

The speed of planning with computers, paired with the supportive mayor of Peabody, who accelerated the approval process as a way to generate sales tax income and jobs, helped control the costs of renovation and shortened the time during which the mall owner was paying off the redevelopment financing.

Skylights, detailed columns and overhead plantings created a more intimate shopping experience than Northshore had offered before.

Graphics, marketing and customer services were also important to redeveloping and remerchandising. During construction, pedestrian bypasses in the arcade were kept accessible, well lit and well signed. Directional signage contained a directory of stores with arrows and was updated at least weekly to keep up with the logistically complex renovation. The renovated mall's logo of a sailboat at sea is carried through on directories, signage and ancillary marketing materials. A customer service desk provides stroller rental, free wheelchair use and mall gift certificates. A shuttle bus provides free transportation to a nearby mall owned by the same developer.

No less a person than the mayor of Peabody has commended the owner on its redevelopment of the mall.

As Mayor Peter Torigan told the Boston Globe: "It will keep people spending in this region. The project has transformed an old mall with a warped floor, an asbestos-filled roof, an unsafe parking lot and grumbling tenants into a skylit mall with granite floors, brass rails, detailed columns, neon lights and oversized stores spanning the retail spectrum."

Storefronts and kiosks catch shoppers' eyes in the renovated Northshore Mall.

Renovation or Expansion of an Existing Project

Owner:
Fox Valley/River Oaks Partnership
Chicago, Illinois

Architect:
James P. Ryan Associates
Farmington Hills, Michigan

Designer:
James P. Ryan Associates
Farmington Hills, Michigan

Certificate of Merit

River Oaks Shopping Center

Calumet City, Illinois United States

Gross size of center:
1,241,853 sq. ft.

Amount of space added or renovated:
180,800 sq. ft.

Gross leasable area excluding anchors:
408,128 sq. ft.

Total acreage of site:
100 acres

Type of center:
Regional center

Physical description:
Enclosed one-level mall

Location of trading area:
Suburban

Population:
- Primary trading area
  1,660,000
- Secondary trading area
  429,000

Development schedule:
- Original opening date
  1966
- Current expansion date
  April 15, 1994

Parking spaces:
- Present number
  6,000

River Oaks Shopping Center, enclosed during the redevelopment, retained an outdoor ambiance through the use of extensive skylights, water features, landscaping and rotations of seasonal flowers.

SEARS
WILSONS
free
layaway
today

Enclosing, expanding and renovating a 1,200,000 sq. ft. superregional mall without closing it was the challenge for the owners, architect and designer of the now-revitalized River Oaks Shopping Center.

The mall was the dominant regional center in Chicago's south suburbs, not particularly threatened by a profusion of strip centers and "big box" centers nearby. But surveys and demographics indicated that significant sales growth was achievable.

Research showed that with only 78 shops, the center lacked a sufficient number of specialty stores to offer meaningful selection options to customers. Because it was an open-air center, shoppers were subjected to the vagaries of Chicago's weather. River Oaks also lacked a food court, customer services commonly found now in regional malls, year-round events and enhanced security.

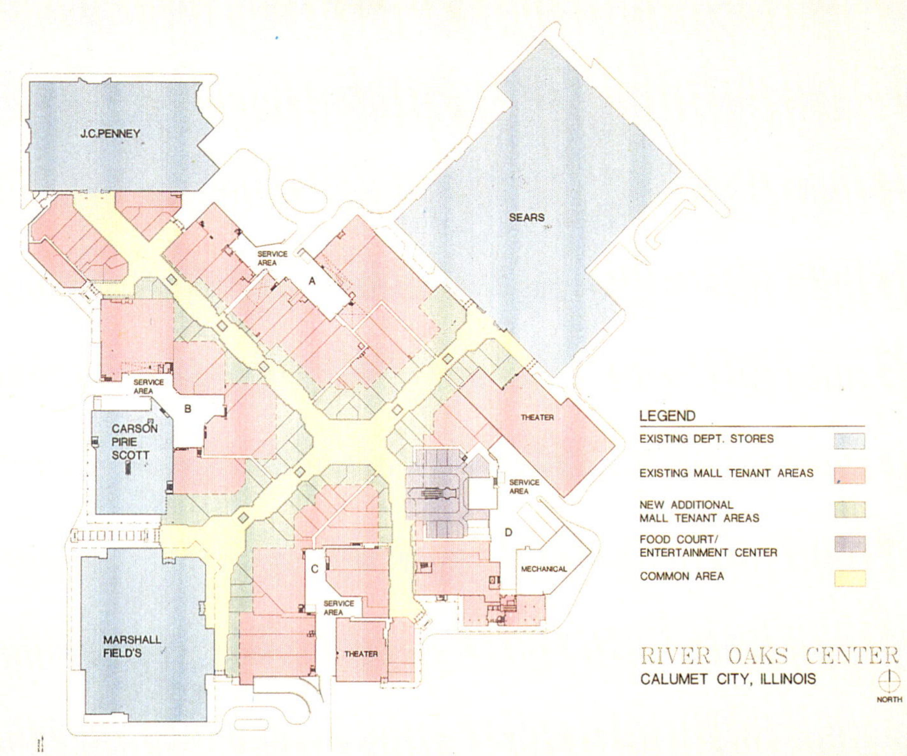

River Oaks Shopping Center became an enclosed mall through renovation, with anchors at three ends and a movie theater at the fourth.

Photo courtesy Peter Fish Studio, Inc. © 1993.

Chicago winters, illustrated in the original open-air center (above), can be ignored inside the new enclosed mall.

Even the basic design concept of the center needed to be changed. Originally, the mall offered a generous parklike setting that, while aesthetically pleasing to many customers, was inappropriate to today's retailing. There was too much distance across the malls, stores were too deep for their narrow storefronts and the mall lacked a strong center court. An opportunity to redevelop presented itself when about 40 percent of the small shops had lease renewals coming up in 1992 and 1993.

The redevelopment plan called for enclosing and in-filling about 180,000 sq. ft. of existing exterior malls and converting this area into a 110,000 sq. ft. interior mall and 70,000 sq. ft. of new retail space. Stores would be retenanted and re-oriented, particularly at the center court. Store count would rise to 110. Maximum store depths would be 115 feet. Two large newer stores just off the center court were relocated to provide space for a new food court and a larger customer service desk.

The River Oaks renovation showed how a drab mall entrance (below) can become exciting (above).

Maintaining the Mall's Parks

To satisfy the many customers who liked the existing parklike malls, the designer retained an outdoor ambience through the use of extensive skylights, water features, landscaping and 17 annual rotations of seasonal flowers.

Open During Renovation

River Oaks was kept open throughout the renovation. The sequence of construction sites was decided by analyzing the required tenant moves, including temporary locations, vacancies and the availability of new space. The plan also called for continuous, convenient, covered customer access to stores, including the relocation of walkways when needed. Enhanced lighting, directional signage, barricades, temporary flooring and noise and dust control were used as well. Good planning made it possible to do only 10 percent of the construction work outside of normal construction hours.

"The Great Mall Makeover"

Communication with tenants and customers was achieved through a two-year marketing plan called "The Great Mall Makeover." Its messages were "We are open for business" and "We are enclosing." Movable customer-friendly animal character signs throughout the mall directed customers to stores. Prominent temporary structures clearly identified mall entries. A new electronic message sign and billboard along the major arterial street reported the progress of the work to the passing public.

Tall signs make mall entrances eminently visible.

MAJOR TENANTS

NAME	TYPE	GLA (SQ. FT.)
Sears	Department store	364,732
Marshall Fields	Department store	263,592
Carson Pirie Scott	Department store	64,936

The renovation retained the center's parklike image.

Benefits of Coordination

The coordination of marketing, construction and leasing plans resulted in a redevelopment effort that not only satisfied retailers and customers, but also kept sales steady through the project, with some stores even experiencing modest increases.

Renovation or Expansion of an Existing Project

Owner:
Chase & Associates
Los Angeles, California

Architect:
Rodney Stutman, AIA, Architects
Tarzana, California

Designer:
Graphic Solutions
San Diego, California
Rodney Stutman, AIA, Architects
Tarzana, California

Certificate of Merit

Spring Street

Long Beach, California
United States

Gross size of center:
100,640 sq. ft.

Amount of space added or renovated:
100,640 sq. ft.

Gross leasable area excluding anchors:
44,462 sq. ft.

Total acreage of site:
7.5 acres

Type of center:
Neighborhood center

Physical description:
Strip center

Location of trading area:
Suburban

Population:
- Primary trading area
  17,973
- Secondary trading area
  164,818

Development schedule:
- Original opening date
  1960
- Current expansion date
  June 1994

Parking spaces:
- Present number
  506

Spring Street's facade was given a sense of dimension by changing forms and volumes, increasing heights of roof lines and interplaying varying geometric shapes and colors.

FOOD 4 LESS

Prior to renovation, Spring Street was known as Plaza Center, an outdated center from the 1960s with a nondescript facade resembling a woodshed. Its virtually uninterrupted length of 850 feet was only one of its problems. By the 1990s, the storefronts had become badly oxidized. Signage was of the old cabinet style. The exteriors of major tenants were virtually indistinguishable from those of small shops. The center also had a vacancy rate of 20 percent, decreasing tenant sales and strong competition just across the street.

In planning the renovation, the architect first sought to break up the long visual line of uninterrupted storefronts. The center's facade was given a sense of dimension by changing forms and volumes, increasing heights of roof lines to the maximum allowable and interplaying varying geometric shapes and colors — which together gave greater identity to small tenants while offering large tenants a dominant presence.

Signage Challenges

The city code would have required signage so small that it would have been difficult to read. Rather than accept the code's limitation, the developer ordered a detailed graphics program that so impressed the city that a sign variance was granted, permitting signage 50 percent larger than code. The new signage used single channel letters, reverse channel letters, exposed neon, open channel neon, and logos and symbols to interpret each tenant's sign.

The renovation introduced various roof countours to the center's stores

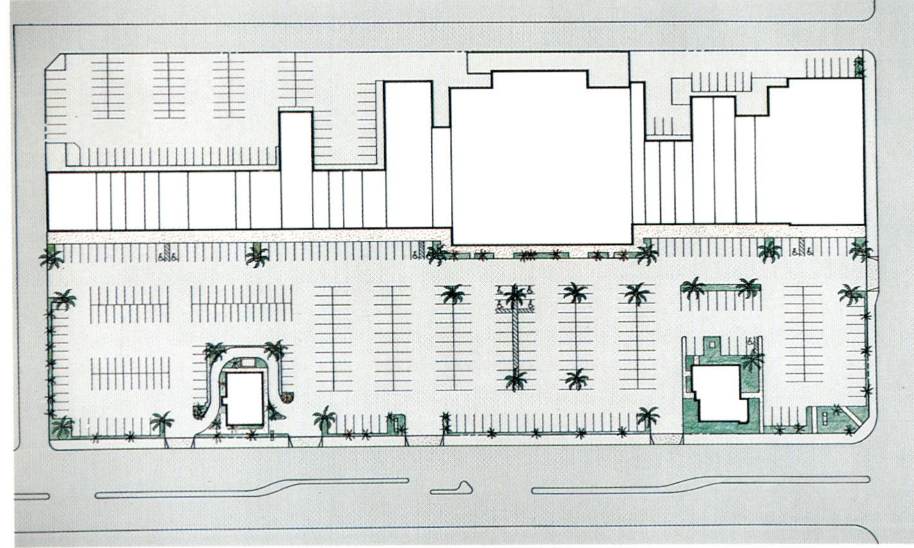

The Spring Street site plan shows the virtually uninterrupted 850-foot stretch of storefront.

Lighting washes center's walls and roofs at night.

MAJOR TENANTS		
NAME	**TYPE**	**GLA (SQ. FT.)**
Food 4 Less	Supermarket	32,134
Thrifty Drug Store	Drugstore	16,452
The Wherehouse Entertainment	Music/video	7,592

"Before" (below) and "after" (above) views illustrate changes in roof design.

By working with tenants and offering subsidies, the developer persuaded all tenants to take part in the signage program, including major national chains such as Thrifty Drug (which uses open channel neon in its secondary signs) and Radio Shack (which uses neon to emphasize electricity bolts in its sign). The two new major pylon signs carry through the signage concept by incorporating bright colors with reverse channel letters, exposed neon and open channel neon.

Three Separate Looks

While many centers have "day" and "night" looks, Spring Street achieves a "twilight" look as well by leaving all open channel neon features lit during daytime hours. Cove lighting washes the walls and slanted roofs at night. In addition to custom lights constructed as accents for the fascia, towering palm trees are lit by well lights. To emphasize the "night" look, hidden roof lights accentuate the various roof contours.

Structural Changes

Structural changes were part of the renovation as well. Unless costly foundation work were to be done, the weight of the new roof heights required lightening the building load. Finished walls, soffits and molding were modified by replacing stucco with an acrylic copolymer. Structural loads from the building frame were lightened by removing the heavy existing concrete roof tile.

Neon draws special attention to storefront signage at night.

Spring Street encouraged retailers to use their store logos within the overall signage concept.

Pylons feature the new Spring Street logo.

Sidewalks Remodeled

Even the sidewalk in front of the stores was remodeled. A new material was used in a special three-process application to cover the old, discolored, cracked concrete. Replacing the concrete would have cost ten times as much as the application. All sidewalk work was done at night with no inconvenience to tenants.

The Transformation

The center remained open during construction, and sales barely fluctuated. All construction areas were barricaded and contained tenant signage with logos. Security guards directed traffic and assured shopper safety. An on-site employee served as liaison to tenants, customers and city officials. Weekly reports to the developer were required of maintenance, landscaping and security crews.

The transformation of bland Plaza Center into the neon-lit Spring Street brought the new center to virtual capacity in leasing and improved sales.

Renovation or Expansion of an Existing Project

Owner:
Compass Retail
Atlanta, Georgia

Architect:
Shapiro Petrauskas Gelber
Philadelphia, Pennsylvania

Certificate of Merit

Westmoreland Mall

Greensburg, Pennsylvania United States

Gross size of center:
1,014,400 sq. ft.

Amount of space added or renovated:
245,300 sq. ft.

Gross leasable area excluding anchors:
661,540 sq. ft.

Total acreage of site:
78 acres

Type of center:
Regional center

Physical description:
Enclosed two-level mall

Location of trading area:
Suburban

Development schedule:
- Original opening date Fall 1973
- Current expansion date May 1994

Parking spaces:
- Present number 6,356

Westmoreland Mall's entrances feature the names of anchor stores as well as the center name.

WESTMORELAND
THE BON·TON
RUBY TUESDAY

A strong shopping destination after its opening in 1973, Westmoreland Mall's visual look and tenant mix had become dated by the early 1990s. Competition had heated up after a major regional traffic artery was built adjacent to a competing mall, prompting further retail development there. An anchor at the competing mall was reported to be unhappy with its management and was considering a move. Finally, surveys showed that Westmoreland's shoppers wanted more food options.

Planned Additions

Responding to these challenges, the owner of Westmoreland Mall planned a major renovation based on a lighter, brighter mall. A new prototype JC Penney would become a fourth anchor. Deck parking would be built connecting to two anchors, replacing parking spaces lost to the JC Penney pad and other new construction. A food court would also be added.

Westmoreland Mall's new site plan shows the location of the four anchor stores.

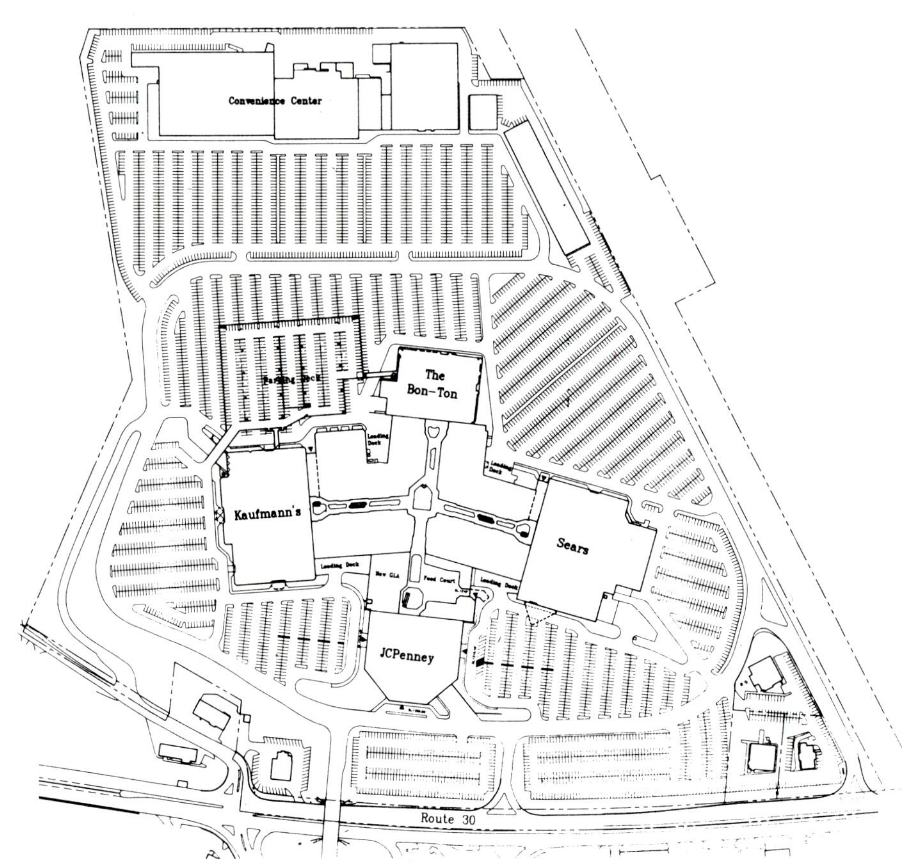

MAJOR TENANTS		
NAME	**TYPE**	**GLA (SQ. FT.)**
Sears	Department store	202,063
Kaufmann's	Department store	169,000
JC Penney	Department store	127,300
The Bon-Ton	Department store	99,800

JC Penney, the new anchor, is highly visible from both the exterior and the interior.

Significantly, and as a way to show the public the revitalized Westmoreland, the new food court and the new JC Penney would be located at the front of the mall, dominating the view from the highway. Other anchors would benefit from the changes by improved circulation and upper-level deck parking bringing shoppers directly to the anchors' doors.

Retenanting focused on appealing to more upper-middle-class shoppers while not alienating Westmoreland's traditional working-class market.

Getting Through the Renovation

The center was open throughout construction. During site work, movable directional signage and part-time "directors" smoothed the flow through temporary traffic patterns. The new parking deck was completed before construction started on the former parking space. Major demolition and structural work were performed at night, with less intrusive work being done during operating hours.

While renovation progressed, the marketing theme "We've Got the Look" was established to communicate the updated architecture and new tenants. Letters and signage kept patrons informed about construction and re-tenanting. Once the entire project was completed, yet another marketing message announced that Westmoreland Mall had "All kinds of shops for all kinds of shoppers," promoting the enhanced tenant mix.

Mall Design Related to Community

Design of the renovated mall was kept in harmony with the community. Unique features remind shoppers of the area's "Steel City" heritage. Classic colors and materials were used throughout, especially for flooring, so that the new storefronts became the main feature of the mall. Special detailing was limited to court areas, and the entire mall was brightened by new skylighted walkways.

Shoppers' eyes are drawn to an elevator at the center court.

Kaufmann's , a center anchor, has signage that commands attention from both levels of Westmoreland Mall.

The food court received special treatment, with strong location signage, tile detail and overhead ribbons combining to create a popular eating destination.

Classic colors were used for flooring lit by natural light.

The new customer service desk is shown before the mall's daily opening.

Increases in Sales

Westmoreland Mall's renovations have satisfied owner, tenants and shoppers alike, bringing about increased post-renovation sales figures in a shopping environment for the 1990s.